50 Russian Dessert Recipes for Home

By: Kelly Johnson

Table of Contents

- Medovik
- Ptichye Moloko
- Syrniki
- Napoleon Cake
- Sharlotka
- Blini
- Kulich
- Pryaniki
- Kissel
- Vatrushka
- Kartoshka
- Ponchiki
- Paskha
- Charlotte Russe
- Zefir
- Chak-Chak
- Oreshki
- Sochnik
- Tvorozhniki
- Kulebyaka
- Kisel
- Keks
- Mazurka
- Gogol-Mogol
- Ruzheiki
- Baranki
- Sukhariki
- Marmelad
- Kulebyaka with Sweet Filling
- Sushki
- Tula Gingerbread
- Far Breton
- Pirog with Sweet Filling
- Solozhenka
- Gnezdo

- Prianik
- Kisel with Berries
- Lazy Vareniki
- Baked Apples with Honey
- Sweet Syrniki with Raisins
- Sweet Curd Dumplings
- Bird's Milk Cake
- Cottage Cheese Pancakes
- Kasha with Berries
- Apple Pie (Yablochny Pirog)
- Sweet Bread Rolls (Bulochki)
- Creamy Semolina Porridge
- Russian Tea Cookies
- Honey Cake
- Lemon Kulich

Medovik

Ingredients:

For the Cake Layers:

- 3/4 cup unsalted butter, softened
- 1 cup granulated sugar
- 4 large eggs
- 2 tablespoons honey
- 1 teaspoon vanilla extract
- 3 1/2 cups all-purpose flour
- 2 teaspoons baking powder
- Pinch of salt

For the Frosting:

- 3 cups heavy cream
- 1 cup powdered sugar
- 1 teaspoon vanilla extract

For Assembly:

- Honey for brushing between layers
- Crushed nuts or grated chocolate for garnish (optional)

Instructions:

1. Prepare the Cake Layers:
    - Preheat your oven to 350°F (175°C). Grease and flour nine 8-inch round cake pans or use fewer pans and bake the layers in batches.
    - In a large mixing bowl, cream together the softened butter and granulated sugar until light and fluffy.
    - Add the eggs, one at a time, beating well after each addition. Then, mix in the honey and vanilla extract until well combined.
    - In a separate bowl, sift together the flour, baking powder, and salt. Gradually add the dry ingredients to the wet ingredients, mixing until a soft dough forms.
    - Divide the dough into 9 equal portions. Roll out each portion between two sheets of parchment paper to about 1/8 inch thickness. Use an 8-inch round cake pan or a template to trim the dough into perfect circles.

- Place each dough circle onto a parchment-lined baking sheet and bake in the preheated oven for 6-8 minutes, or until lightly golden brown. Repeat until all dough portions are baked.
2. Make the Frosting:
    - In a large mixing bowl, beat the heavy cream, powdered sugar, and vanilla extract together until stiff peaks form. Be careful not to overbeat.
3. Assemble the Cake:
    - Once the cake layers are completely cooled, place one layer on a serving plate or cake stand. Brush the top with a thin layer of honey.
    - Spread a generous layer of frosting over the cake layer. Repeat with the remaining cake layers, honey, and frosting, stacking them on top of each other.
    - Use the remaining frosting to cover the top and sides of the cake.
    - Refrigerate the cake for at least 6 hours or overnight to allow the flavors to meld and the frosting to set.
4. Decorate the Cake:
    - Before serving, garnish the top of the cake with crushed nuts or grated chocolate, if desired.
    - Slice and serve the Medovik cake, and enjoy!

Tips:

- Make sure to roll out the dough for each layer thinly and evenly to ensure uniform baking.
- Be patient when assembling the cake, allowing each layer to chill in the refrigerator before adding the next layer. This will help prevent the cake from collapsing.
- You can adjust the sweetness of the frosting by adding more or less powdered sugar according to your preference.
- Store any leftover Medovik cake in the refrigerator for up to 3 days.

Enjoy this delicious and indulgent Russian Honey Cake as a delightful dessert for special occasions or gatherings!

Ptichye Moloko

Ingredients:

For the Sponge Cake:

- 4 large eggs
- 1 cup granulated sugar
- 1 teaspoon vanilla extract
- 1 cup all-purpose flour
- 1 teaspoon baking powder
- Pinch of salt

For the Marshmallow Filling:

- 1 cup granulated sugar
- 1/4 cup water
- 2 tablespoons gelatin powder
- 1/4 cup cold water
- 4 large egg whites
- Pinch of salt
- 1 teaspoon vanilla extract

For Assembly and Coating:

- 8 ounces dark chocolate, chopped
- 2 tablespoons vegetable oil

Instructions:

1. Prepare the Sponge Cake:
    - Preheat your oven to 350°F (175°C). Grease and line a 9x13-inch baking pan with parchment paper.
    - In a large mixing bowl, beat the eggs and granulated sugar together with an electric mixer until pale and fluffy. Stir in the vanilla extract.
    - In a separate bowl, sift together the flour, baking powder, and salt. Gradually add the dry ingredients to the egg mixture, folding gently until just combined.
    - Pour the batter into the prepared baking pan and spread it out evenly.

- Bake in the preheated oven for 20-25 minutes, or until the cake is golden brown and springs back when lightly touched. Remove from the oven and let it cool completely.
2. Make the Marshmallow Filling:
    - In a small saucepan, combine the granulated sugar and 1/4 cup water. Cook over medium heat, stirring occasionally, until the sugar has dissolved and the mixture reaches 240°F (115°C) on a candy thermometer.
    - Meanwhile, sprinkle the gelatin powder over 1/4 cup cold water in a small bowl and let it soften for about 5 minutes.
    - In a large mixing bowl, beat the egg whites and a pinch of salt with an electric mixer until soft peaks form.
    - Gradually pour the hot sugar syrup into the beaten egg whites, beating continuously until stiff, glossy peaks form.
    - Microwave the softened gelatin mixture for 15-20 seconds, or until melted. Slowly pour it into the marshmallow mixture, beating continuously until well combined. Stir in the vanilla extract.
3. Assemble the Ptichye Moloko:
    - Cut the cooled sponge cake into squares or rectangles, depending on your preference.
    - Place the cake squares on a wire rack set over a baking sheet to catch any drips. Spoon the marshmallow filling over the cake squares, spreading it out evenly with a spatula.
    - Refrigerate the assembled cakes for at least 1 hour, or until the marshmallow filling is set.
4. Coat with Chocolate:
    - In a heatproof bowl set over a pot of simmering water, melt the chopped chocolate and vegetable oil together, stirring until smooth.
    - Dip each chilled cake square into the melted chocolate, coating it completely. Place it back on the wire rack to allow any excess chocolate to drip off.
    - Return the coated cakes to the refrigerator for about 30 minutes, or until the chocolate is set.
5. Serve and Enjoy:
    - Once the chocolate coating is set, serve the Ptichye moloko cakes and enjoy!

Tips:

- You can customize the flavor of the sponge cake by adding lemon zest or orange zest for a citrusy twist.
- Be sure to work quickly when dipping the cakes into the melted chocolate to prevent the marshmallow filling from melting.
- Store any leftover Ptichye moloko cakes in an airtight container in the refrigerator for up to 3 days.

Enjoy these homemade Ptichye moloko cakes as a delicious and decadent treat reminiscent of Russian confectionery!

Syrniki

Ingredients:

- 2 cups farmer's cheese (quark or tvorog), well-drained
- 2 large eggs
- 1/4 cup granulated sugar
- 1 teaspoon vanilla extract
- 1/2 teaspoon salt
- 1 cup all-purpose flour, plus more as needed
- Vegetable oil, for frying
- Sour cream, jam, honey, or fresh berries, for serving

Instructions:

1. Prepare the Farmer's Cheese:
   - If your farmer's cheese is very wet, place it in a fine-mesh strainer set over a bowl and let it drain for about 30 minutes to remove excess moisture.
2. Mix the Batter:
   - In a large mixing bowl, combine the drained farmer's cheese, eggs, granulated sugar, vanilla extract, and salt. Mix until well combined.
   - Gradually add the flour, stirring until a soft and slightly sticky dough forms. The dough should be thick enough to hold its shape but not too dry.
3. Form the Pancakes:
   - Lightly flour your hands and a clean work surface. Take a portion of the dough and roll it into a ball, then flatten it slightly to form a pancake about 1/2 inch thick. Repeat with the remaining dough, shaping it into pancakes.
4. Fry the Syrniki:
   - Heat a skillet or frying pan over medium heat and add enough vegetable oil to coat the bottom.
   - Once the oil is hot, carefully place the syrniki in the pan, leaving some space between each one. Cook in batches if necessary.
   - Fry the syrniki for 3-4 minutes on each side, or until they are golden brown and cooked through. Adjust the heat as needed to prevent them from burning.
   - Transfer the cooked syrniki to a paper towel-lined plate to drain excess oil.
5. Serve:
   - Serve the syrniki warm, topped with sour cream, jam, honey, or fresh berries, as desired.

Tips:

- If you prefer a sweeter flavor, you can increase the amount of sugar in the batter.
- Feel free to customize your syrniki by adding ingredients like lemon zest, cinnamon, or raisins to the batter.
- To keep the syrniki warm while you cook the remaining batches, place them on a baking sheet in a low oven (around 200°F or 90°C) until ready to serve.

Enjoy these homemade syrniki as a delightful and comforting breakfast or dessert option!

Napoleon Cake

Ingredients:

For the Pastry Cream:

- 2 cups whole milk
- 1/2 cup granulated sugar
- 4 large egg yolks
- 1/4 cup cornstarch
- 2 tablespoons unsalted butter
- 1 teaspoon vanilla extract

For Assembly:

- 1 package (17.3 ounces) puff pastry, thawed according to package instructions
- Confectioners' sugar, for dusting

Instructions:

1. Prepare the Pastry Cream:
    - In a saucepan, heat the milk over medium heat until it just begins to simmer. Remove from heat.
    - In a mixing bowl, whisk together the sugar, egg yolks, and cornstarch until well combined and slightly thickened.
    - Gradually pour the hot milk into the egg mixture, whisking constantly to temper the eggs.
    - Return the mixture to the saucepan and cook over medium heat, stirring constantly, until it thickens and comes to a boil.
    - Remove from heat and stir in the butter and vanilla extract until smooth. Transfer the pastry cream to a bowl, cover with plastic wrap (pressing the wrap directly onto the surface to prevent a skin from forming), and refrigerate until completely chilled.
2. Prepare the Puff Pastry:
    - Preheat your oven to 400°F (200°C). Line two baking sheets with parchment paper.
    - Roll out the puff pastry on a lightly floured surface into two 12x12-inch squares. Transfer the pastry squares to the prepared baking sheets.
    - Prick the surface of the pastry squares all over with a fork to prevent them from puffing up too much during baking.

- Bake the pastry squares in the preheated oven for 15-20 minutes, or until golden brown and crispy. Remove from the oven and let them cool completely on wire racks.
3. Assemble the Napoleon Cake:
    - Once the pastry cream and puff pastry are completely cooled, place one of the pastry squares on a serving platter.
    - Spread a layer of pastry cream evenly over the pastry square, using about half of the pastry cream.
    - Place the second pastry square on top of the cream and gently press down.
    - Spread the remaining pastry cream evenly over the top of the second pastry square.
    - Refrigerate the assembled cake for at least 1 hour to allow the pastry cream to set.
4. Finish and Serve:
    - Before serving, dust the top of the Napoleon cake with confectioners' sugar.
    - Use a sharp knife to slice the cake into squares or rectangles, and serve chilled.

Tips:

- For a decorative touch, you can use a fork to create a crisscross pattern on top of the pastry squares before baking.
- To make the assembly process easier, you can cut the pastry squares into smaller rectangles or squares before adding the pastry cream.
- Napoleon cake is best served chilled and can be stored in the refrigerator for up to 2 days.

Enjoy this classic Napoleon cake with its layers of crispy puff pastry and creamy pastry cream for a delicious and elegant dessert!

Sharlotka

Ingredients:

- 4 large eggs
- 1 cup granulated sugar
- 1 teaspoon vanilla extract
- 1 cup all-purpose flour
- 1 teaspoon baking powder
- Pinch of salt
- 4-5 medium apples, peeled, cored, and thinly sliced
- Powdered sugar, for dusting (optional)
- Ground cinnamon, for dusting (optional)

Instructions:

1. Preheat the Oven:
    - Preheat your oven to 350°F (175°C). Grease a 9-inch round cake pan and line the bottom with parchment paper for easy removal.
2. Prepare the Batter:
    - In a large mixing bowl, beat the eggs and granulated sugar together until pale and fluffy. Add the vanilla extract and mix until combined.
    - In a separate bowl, sift together the flour, baking powder, and salt. Gradually add the dry ingredients to the egg mixture, mixing until smooth and well combined.
3. Add the Apples:
    - Gently fold the thinly sliced apples into the batter until evenly coated.
4. Bake the Cake:
    - Pour the batter into the prepared cake pan and spread it out evenly with a spatula.
    - Bake in the preheated oven for 40-45 minutes, or until the cake is golden brown and a toothpick inserted into the center comes out clean.
5. Cool and Serve:
    - Remove the cake from the oven and let it cool in the pan for about 10 minutes. Then, carefully transfer it to a wire rack to cool completely.
    - Once cooled, dust the top of the Sharlotka with powdered sugar and ground cinnamon, if desired.
    - Slice and serve the Sharlotka cake, either warm or at room temperature.

Tips:

- You can use any variety of apples for this recipe, but tart apples like Granny Smith or Jonathan work particularly well.
- For added flavor, you can sprinkle the sliced apples with a little lemon juice and cinnamon before folding them into the batter.
- Sharlotka is traditionally served plain or with a dollop of whipped cream or vanilla ice cream on the side.
- Leftover Sharlotka can be stored in an airtight container at room temperature for up to 2 days or in the refrigerator for longer storage.

Enjoy this simple and delicious Sharlotka cake as a comforting treat with a cup of tea or coffee!

Blini

Ingredients:

- 1 cup all-purpose flour
- 1 1/2 cups whole milk
- 2 large eggs
- 2 tablespoons unsalted butter, melted
- 1 tablespoon granulated sugar (for sweet blini, optional)
- 1/4 teaspoon salt
- Additional butter or oil for cooking

Instructions:

1. Prepare the Batter:
    - In a mixing bowl, whisk together the flour, sugar (if using), and salt.
    - In a separate bowl, beat the eggs, then add the milk and melted butter. Whisk until well combined.
    - Gradually add the wet ingredients to the dry ingredients, whisking until smooth. The batter should be thin and pourable.
2. Rest the Batter:
    - Let the batter rest for about 30 minutes at room temperature. This allows the flour to fully hydrate and helps develop a smoother texture.
3. Cook the Blini:
    - Heat a non-stick skillet or crepe pan over medium heat. Add a small amount of butter or oil to lightly grease the pan.
    - Pour about 1/4 cup of batter into the center of the pan, swirling it around to spread it into a thin, even layer.
    - Cook the blini for 1-2 minutes, or until the edges start to curl up and the bottom is lightly golden brown.
    - Flip the blini using a spatula and cook for an additional 1-2 minutes on the other side, until golden brown and cooked through.
    - Repeat with the remaining batter, greasing the pan as needed between each blini.
4. Serve:
    - Serve the blini warm, either folded or rolled, with your choice of toppings.
    - For sweet blini, you can serve them with honey, jam, fresh berries, whipped cream, or sweetened condensed milk.

- For savory blini, you can serve them with sour cream, smoked salmon, caviar, cream cheese, or sautéed mushrooms.

Tips:

- To keep the blini warm while you cook the remaining batch, you can place them on a baking sheet in a low oven (around 200°F or 90°C) until ready to serve.
- If you prefer a smoother texture, you can strain the batter through a fine-mesh sieve before cooking the blini.
- Adjust the thickness of the blini by adding more or less batter to the pan and spreading it out accordingly.

Enjoy these versatile and delicious blini as a classic Russian treat for breakfast, brunch, or any time of day!

Kulich

Ingredients:

For the Bread:

- 4 cups all-purpose flour
- 1/2 cup granulated sugar
- 1/2 teaspoon salt
- 1 packet (2 1/4 teaspoons) active dry yeast
- 1/2 cup whole milk, warmed to about 110°F (45°C)
- 1/2 cup unsalted butter, melted and cooled
- 3 large eggs, beaten
- 1/2 teaspoon vanilla extract
- Zest of 1 lemon or orange
- 1/2 cup mixed dried fruits (such as raisins, currants, or chopped apricots)
- 1/2 cup chopped nuts (such as almonds, walnuts, or pecans)
- 1/2 teaspoon ground cardamom (optional)
- 1/4 teaspoon ground nutmeg (optional)

For the Glaze (optional):

- 1 cup powdered sugar
- 2-3 tablespoons whole milk
- 1/2 teaspoon vanilla extract
- Slivered almonds, candied fruit, or sprinkles for decoration (optional)

Instructions:

1. Prepare the Dough:
    - In a large mixing bowl, combine the flour, sugar, salt, and yeast. Make a well in the center.
    - Pour the warm milk, melted butter, beaten eggs, vanilla extract, and citrus zest into the well. Mix until a soft dough forms.
    - Knead the dough on a floured surface for about 5-7 minutes, or until smooth and elastic. Alternatively, you can use a stand mixer fitted with a dough hook attachment.
    - Transfer the dough to a greased bowl, cover with a clean kitchen towel or plastic wrap, and let it rise in a warm place until doubled in size, about 1-2 hours.

2. Add the Fruits and Nuts:
    - Once the dough has risen, gently punch it down to deflate. Add the dried fruits, chopped nuts, and spices (if using), and knead until evenly distributed throughout the dough.
3. Shape the Kulich:
    - Divide the dough into two equal portions. Shape each portion into a tall cylindrical loaf and place them in greased and floured Kulich molds or tall, greased, and floured coffee cans. Alternatively, you can use parchment paper-lined baking pans.
    - Cover the molds or pans with a clean kitchen towel and let the dough rise again until doubled in size, about 1-2 hours.
4. Bake the Kulich:
    - Preheat your oven to 350°F (175°C). Bake the Kulich in the preheated oven for 30-40 minutes, or until golden brown and cooked through. If the tops start to brown too quickly, cover them loosely with aluminum foil.
    - Remove the Kulich from the oven and let them cool in the molds or pans for a few minutes before transferring them to wire racks to cool completely.
5. Glaze and Decorate (optional):
    - Once the Kulich have cooled completely, you can glaze them by whisking together the powdered sugar, milk, and vanilla extract until smooth. Drizzle the glaze over the Kulich and decorate with slivered almonds, candied fruit, or sprinkles, if desired.
6. Serve and Enjoy:
    - Slice and serve the Kulich as a delicious Easter treat. It's traditionally enjoyed with Paskha (Russian Easter cheesecake) and colored eggs.

Tips:

- Make sure your yeast is fresh and active for the best rise.
- You can customize the dried fruits and nuts according to your preference.
- If you don't have Kulich molds or coffee cans, you can use tall parchment paper-lined baking pans.
- Store leftover Kulich in an airtight container at room temperature for up to 3 days, or freeze for longer storage.

Enjoy making and sharing this traditional Russian Easter bread with your friends and family!

Pryaniki

Ingredients:

For the Cookies:

- 2 cups all-purpose flour
- 1/2 teaspoon baking soda
- 1/2 teaspoon ground cinnamon
- 1/2 teaspoon ground ginger
- 1/4 teaspoon ground cloves
- 1/4 teaspoon ground nutmeg
- 1/4 teaspoon salt
- 1/2 cup unsalted butter, softened
- 1/2 cup granulated sugar
- 1/2 cup honey
- 1 large egg

For the Glaze:

- 1 cup powdered sugar
- 2-3 tablespoons whole milk
- 1/2 teaspoon vanilla extract

Instructions:

1. Prepare the Dough:
    - In a medium mixing bowl, whisk together the flour, baking soda, ground cinnamon, ginger, cloves, nutmeg, and salt until well combined.
    - In a separate large mixing bowl, cream together the softened butter and granulated sugar until light and fluffy. Add the honey and egg, and mix until smooth.
    - Gradually add the dry ingredients to the wet ingredients, mixing until a soft dough forms. If the dough is too sticky, you can add a little more flour as needed.
    - Wrap the dough in plastic wrap and refrigerate for at least 1 hour, or until firm.
2. Preheat the Oven:
    - Preheat your oven to 350°F (175°C). Line a baking sheet with parchment paper or silicone baking mats.

3. Shape the Cookies:
    - On a lightly floured surface, roll out the chilled dough to about 1/4 inch thickness. Use cookie cutters to cut out shapes or simply roll the dough into balls and flatten slightly.
    - Place the shaped cookies on the prepared baking sheet, leaving a little space between each one.
4. Bake the Cookies:
    - Bake the cookies in the preheated oven for 8-10 minutes, or until the edges are lightly golden brown.
    - Remove the cookies from the oven and let them cool on the baking sheet for a few minutes before transferring them to wire racks to cool completely.
5. Prepare the Glaze:
    - In a small mixing bowl, whisk together the powdered sugar, milk, and vanilla extract until smooth. Adjust the consistency by adding more milk if needed.
6. Glaze the Cookies:
    - Once the cookies are completely cooled, drizzle the glaze over the top of each cookie using a spoon or icing bag.
    - Allow the glaze to set before serving or storing the cookies.

Tips:

- Feel free to adjust the spices according to your taste preferences. You can also add other spices like cardamom or allspice for additional flavor.
- For a softer texture, roll the dough out slightly thicker. For crispier cookies, roll the dough out thinner.
- Pryaniki can be stored in an airtight container at room temperature for up to a week. You can also freeze them for longer storage.

Enjoy these homemade pryaniki cookies as a delicious and aromatic treat with a cup of tea or coffee!

Kissel

Ingredients:

- 2 cups fruit juice (such as berry juice, cherry juice, or apple juice)
- 1/4 cup granulated sugar (adjust to taste)
- 3 tablespoons cornstarch or potato starch
- 1/4 cup cold water
- Fresh fruit or berries for garnish (optional)

Instructions:

1. Prepare the Fruit Juice:
    - If you're using fresh fruit, wash and prepare the fruit by removing any stems, seeds, or pits. Place the fruit in a blender or food processor and blend until smooth. Strain the fruit puree through a fine-mesh sieve to remove any solids, yielding fruit juice.
    - If you're using store-bought fruit juice, simply measure out the desired amount.
2. Combine the Ingredients:
    - In a saucepan, combine the fruit juice and granulated sugar. Heat the mixture over medium heat, stirring occasionally, until the sugar has dissolved and the mixture is hot but not boiling.
3. Thicken the Kissel:
    - In a small bowl, mix the cornstarch or potato starch with the cold water until smooth, creating a slurry.
    - Gradually pour the starch slurry into the hot fruit juice mixture, whisking constantly to prevent lumps from forming.
4. Cook the Kissel:
    - Continue to cook the mixture over medium heat, stirring constantly, until it thickens and reaches a pudding-like consistency. This should take about 3-5 minutes.
5. Cool and Serve:
    - Remove the saucepan from the heat and let the kissel cool slightly.
    - Transfer the kissel to individual serving bowls or glasses and refrigerate until completely chilled and set, about 1-2 hours.
6. Garnish and Enjoy:
    - Before serving, you can garnish the kissel with fresh fruit or berries, if desired.

- Serve the chilled kissel as a refreshing and light dessert on its own, or with a dollop of whipped cream or yogurt on top.

Tips:

- You can adjust the sweetness of the kissel by adding more or less sugar according to your taste preferences.
- Experiment with different fruit juices and combinations to create unique flavors of kissel.
- If you prefer a smoother texture, you can blend the fruit juice with the starch slurry before heating it on the stove.
- Leftover kissel can be stored in the refrigerator for up to 3 days.

Enjoy this simple and delicious homemade kissel as a refreshing dessert or snack!

Vatrushka

Ingredients:

For the Dough:

- 2 1/4 teaspoons (1 packet) active dry yeast
- 1/4 cup warm water (about 110°F)
- 1/2 cup whole milk, warmed
- 1/4 cup granulated sugar
- 1/4 cup unsalted butter, melted
- 2 large eggs
- 1 teaspoon vanilla extract
- 3 1/2 cups all-purpose flour
- 1/2 teaspoon salt

For the Filling:

- 1 pound farmer's cheese (tvorog), well-drained
- 1/4 cup granulated sugar
- 1 large egg
- 1/2 teaspoon vanilla extract
- Optional: 1/2 cup raisins, soaked in warm water and drained

For Egg Wash:

- 1 large egg, beaten with 1 tablespoon water

Instructions:

1. Prepare the Dough:
    - In a small bowl, dissolve the yeast in warm water and let it sit for about 5 minutes, or until foamy.
    - In a large mixing bowl or the bowl of a stand mixer, combine the warm milk, sugar, melted butter, eggs, and vanilla extract. Mix well.
    - Add the yeast mixture to the bowl and stir to combine.
    - Gradually add the flour and salt to the wet ingredients, mixing until a soft dough forms.
    - Knead the dough on a floured surface or with the dough hook attachment of a stand mixer for about 5-7 minutes, or until smooth and elastic.

- Place the dough in a greased bowl, cover with a clean kitchen towel or plastic wrap, and let it rise in a warm place until doubled in size, about 1-2 hours.
2. Prepare the Filling:
   - In a mixing bowl, combine the farmer's cheese, granulated sugar, egg, and vanilla extract. Mix until well combined. If using raisins, gently fold them into the cheese mixture.
3. Shape the Vatrushka:
   - Once the dough has risen, punch it down to deflate. Divide the dough into equal-sized portions and shape them into balls.
   - Place the dough balls on a parchment-lined baking sheet, leaving some space between each one.
   - Flatten each dough ball slightly with your palm to create a depression in the center.
   - Fill each depression with a spoonful of the cheese filling, spreading it out slightly.
4. Let Rise Again:
   - Cover the filled vatrushka with a clean kitchen towel and let them rise for another 30-45 minutes, or until slightly puffy.
5. Bake the Vatrushka:
   - Preheat your oven to 375°F (190°C). Brush the tops of the vatrushka with the egg wash.
   - Bake in the preheated oven for 15-20 minutes, or until golden brown.
   - Remove from the oven and let them cool on a wire rack before serving.
6. Serve and Enjoy:
   - Vatrushka can be served warm or at room temperature. Enjoy them as a delicious breakfast pastry or snack.

Tips:

- If you can't find farmer's cheese (tvorog), you can use a combination of ricotta cheese and cottage cheese as a substitute.
- You can customize the filling by adding ingredients like lemon zest, cinnamon, or chopped nuts for extra flavor.
- Store leftover vatrushka in an airtight container at room temperature for up to 2 days, or in the refrigerator for longer storage. Reheat briefly in the oven or microwave before serving, if desired.

Enjoy these delightful vatrushka pastries with their creamy cheese filling and soft, fluffy dough!

Kartoshka

Ingredients:

- 200g (about 7 oz) tea biscuits or plain cookies (such as digestive biscuits or graham crackers)
- 100g (about 3.5 oz) unsalted butter, softened
- 1/4 cup unsweetened cocoa powder, plus more for rolling
- 1/2 cup sweetened condensed milk
- 1 teaspoon vanilla extract
- Grated chocolate or cocoa powder for decoration (optional)

Instructions:

1. Prepare the Cookies:
   - Place the cookies in a food processor or blender and pulse until finely crushed. Alternatively, you can place the cookies in a resealable plastic bag and crush them with a rolling pin.
2. Make the Kartoshka Mixture:
   - In a mixing bowl, combine the crushed cookies, softened butter, cocoa powder, sweetened condensed milk, and vanilla extract. Mix until well combined and the mixture holds together.
3. Shape the Kartoshka:
   - Take small portions of the mixture and roll them into small potato-shaped balls with your hands. The size can vary, but they are typically about the size of a walnut.
4. Roll in Cocoa Powder:
   - Roll each kartoshka ball in cocoa powder until evenly coated. This gives them their characteristic "potato" appearance.
5. Decorate (Optional):
   - If desired, you can press a piece of chopped chocolate or a small nut into the top of each kartoshka to resemble a potato "sprout."
6. Chill and Serve:
   - Place the kartoshka on a baking sheet lined with parchment paper and refrigerate for at least 1-2 hours, or until firm.
   - Once chilled, transfer the kartoshka to a serving platter and enjoy as a delicious and nostalgic treat.

Tips:

- You can customize the flavor of kartoshka by adding ingredients like chopped nuts, dried fruits, or rum extract to the mixture.
- For a richer flavor, you can substitute part of the cocoa powder with melted chocolate.
- Store leftover kartoshka in an airtight container in the refrigerator for up to 1 week.

Enjoy making and sharing these delightful kartoshka treats with friends and family!

Ponchiki

Ingredients:

- 2 1/4 teaspoons (1 packet) active dry yeast
- 1/4 cup warm water (about 110°F)
- 3/4 cup whole milk, warmed
- 1/4 cup granulated sugar
- 1/4 cup unsalted butter, melted
- 2 large eggs
- 1 teaspoon vanilla extract
- 1/2 teaspoon salt
- 3 1/2 cups all-purpose flour, plus more for dusting
- Vegetable oil for frying
- Powdered sugar for dusting

Instructions:

1. Activate the Yeast:
    - In a small bowl, dissolve the yeast in warm water and let it sit for about 5 minutes, or until foamy.
2. Make the Dough:
    - In a large mixing bowl or the bowl of a stand mixer, combine the warm milk, sugar, melted butter, eggs, vanilla extract, and salt. Mix well.
    - Add the activated yeast mixture to the bowl and stir to combine.
    - Gradually add the flour to the wet ingredients, mixing until a soft dough forms.
    - Knead the dough on a floured surface or with the dough hook attachment of a stand mixer for about 5-7 minutes, or until smooth and elastic.
    - Place the dough in a greased bowl, cover with a clean kitchen towel or plastic wrap, and let it rise in a warm place until doubled in size, about 1-2 hours.
3. Shape and Fry the Ponchiki:
    - Once the dough has risen, punch it down to deflate. Turn it out onto a floured surface and roll it out to about 1/2 inch thickness.
    - Use a round cookie cutter or drinking glass to cut out small circles of dough. You can also use your hands to shape the dough into small balls.
    - Place the dough circles or balls on a parchment-lined baking sheet and cover with a clean kitchen towel. Let them rise for another 30 minutes.

4. Fry the Ponchiki:
   - In a large, heavy-bottomed pot or deep fryer, heat vegetable oil to 350°F (175°C).
   - Carefully place a few ponchiki in the hot oil, being careful not to overcrowd the pot. Fry for 2-3 minutes per side, or until golden brown and cooked through.
   - Use a slotted spoon or spider to remove the fried ponchiki from the oil and transfer them to a paper towel-lined plate to drain excess oil. Repeat with the remaining dough.
5. Serve and Enjoy:
   - Once the ponchiki are cool enough to handle, dust them generously with powdered sugar.
   - Serve the ponchiki warm as a delicious treat for breakfast, dessert, or anytime snack.

Tips:

- You can fill the ponchiki with jam or sweetened condensed milk by using a piping bag with a small tip to inject the filling into the center of each doughnut after frying.
- For a richer flavor, you can add lemon zest or orange zest to the dough.
- Store leftover ponchiki in an airtight container at room temperature for up to 2 days. Reheat briefly in the microwave or oven before serving, if desired.

Enjoy making and indulging in these delightful homemade ponchiki!

Paskha

Ingredients:

- 1 pound farmer's cheese (tvorog), well-drained
- 1/2 cup unsalted butter, softened
- 1 cup granulated sugar
- 4 large eggs, separated
- 1/2 cup sour cream or heavy cream
- 1 teaspoon vanilla extract
- 1/2 cup mixed candied fruit, chopped nuts, or raisins (optional)
- Confectioners' sugar for dusting (optional)
- Decorations such as crosses, flowers, or "XB" made from candied fruit or nuts (optional)

Instructions:

1. Prepare the Farmer's Cheese:
   - If the farmer's cheese is wet, place it in a fine-mesh sieve set over a bowl and let it drain in the refrigerator for several hours or overnight.
2. Mix the Ingredients:
   - In a large mixing bowl, cream together the softened butter and granulated sugar until light and fluffy.
   - Add the egg yolks one at a time, beating well after each addition.
   - Stir in the drained farmer's cheese, sour cream or heavy cream, and vanilla extract until well combined.
   - If using, fold in the candied fruit, chopped nuts, or raisins.
3. Whip the Egg Whites:
   - In a separate clean mixing bowl, beat the egg whites until stiff peaks form.
   - Gently fold the beaten egg whites into the cheese mixture until evenly incorporated.
4. Mold the Paskha:
   - Line a Paskha mold or a clean, empty 1-pound food can (with both ends removed) with plastic wrap, leaving some overhang.
   - Spoon the Paskha mixture into the prepared mold, pressing it down firmly and smoothing the top with a spatula.
   - Fold the overhanging plastic wrap over the top of the Paskha to cover it completely.

- Place a weight on top of the Paskha (such as a can of food) and refrigerate for at least 6 hours or overnight to set.
5. Decorate and Serve:
    - Once set, carefully unmold the Paskha onto a serving plate.
    - If desired, decorate the Paskha with crosses, flowers, or the letters "XB" made from candied fruit or nuts.
    - Dust the top of the Paskha with confectioners' sugar before serving, if desired.
6. Enjoy:
    - Slice and serve the Paskha as a traditional Easter dessert, accompanied by kulich (Easter bread) and colored eggs.

Tips:

- You can adjust the sweetness of the Paskha by adding more or less sugar according to your taste preference.
- For a smoother texture, you can press the cheese mixture through a fine-mesh sieve before mixing it with the other ingredients.
- Leftover Paskha can be stored in the refrigerator for up to 3 days. Allow it to come to room temperature before serving for the best flavor and texture.

Enjoy this delicious and festive Russian Easter dessert with your family and friends!

Charlotte Russe

Ingredients:

For the Sponge Cake Base:

- 1 package of ladyfingers or sponge cake
- 1/2 cup simple syrup (optional, for moistening the cake)

For the Bavarian Cream Filling:

- 2 cups heavy cream
- 1/2 cup granulated sugar
- 1 tablespoon unflavored gelatin
- 2 tablespoons cold water
- 4 large egg yolks
- 1 teaspoon vanilla extract

For the Topping:

- 1 cup heavy cream
- 2 tablespoons powdered sugar
- Fresh berries, chocolate shavings, or other garnishes (optional)

Instructions:

1. Prepare the Sponge Cake Base:
   - If using ladyfingers, line the bottom and sides of a springform pan with them, standing them up vertically. If using sponge cake, cut it into strips and line the pan with them.
   - Optional: Drizzle the sponge cake with simple syrup to moisten it.
2. Make the Bavarian Cream Filling:
   - In a small bowl, sprinkle the gelatin over the cold water and let it sit for a few minutes to soften.
   - In a medium saucepan, whisk together the egg yolks and sugar until pale and thick. Gradually whisk in 1 cup of the heavy cream.
   - Place the saucepan over medium heat and cook, stirring constantly, until the mixture thickens and coats the back of a spoon (about 5-7 minutes). Do not let it boil.
   - Remove the saucepan from the heat and stir in the softened gelatin until completely dissolved. Stir in the vanilla extract.

- Transfer the mixture to a bowl and let it cool to room temperature.
3. Whip the Cream:
   - In a separate bowl, whip the remaining 1 cup of heavy cream until stiff peaks form.
   - Gently fold the whipped cream into the cooled Bavarian cream mixture until well combined.
4. Assemble the Charlotte Russe:
   - Pour the Bavarian cream filling into the prepared pan, smoothing the top with a spatula.
   - Cover the pan with plastic wrap and refrigerate for at least 4 hours or until set.
5. Prepare the Topping:
   - Before serving, whip the remaining cup of heavy cream with powdered sugar until stiff peaks form.
   - Spread the whipped cream over the top of the set Bavarian cream.
6. Garnish and Serve:
   - Garnish the Charlotte Russe with fresh berries, chocolate shavings, or other toppings of your choice.
   - Slice and serve chilled.

Enjoy this elegant and delicious Charlotte Russe as a delightful dessert for special occasions or gatherings!

Zefir

Ingredients:

- 1 1/2 cups fruit puree (such as apple, berry, or a mix)
- 1 1/2 cups granulated sugar
- 1 tablespoon agar-agar powder
- 1/2 cup water
- 2 large egg whites, at room temperature
- 1/2 teaspoon vanilla extract
- Powdered sugar for dusting

Instructions:

1. Prepare the Fruit Puree:
    - If you're using fresh fruit, puree the fruit in a blender or food processor until smooth. Strain the puree through a fine-mesh sieve to remove any seeds or pulp. Measure out 1 1/2 cups of the fruit puree.
2. Prepare the Agar-Agar Mixture:
    - In a small saucepan, combine the agar-agar powder and water. Stir well to dissolve the agar-agar. Let it sit for about 5 minutes to bloom.
3. Cook the Fruit Puree and Sugar:
    - In a larger saucepan, combine the fruit puree and granulated sugar. Heat the mixture over medium heat, stirring constantly until the sugar dissolves and the mixture begins to simmer. Continue cooking for another 2-3 minutes.
4. Add the Agar-Agar:
    - Add the agar-agar mixture to the saucepan with the fruit puree and sugar. Stir continuously and bring to a boil. Cook for about 1-2 minutes until the mixture thickens. Remove from heat and let it cool slightly.
5. Beat the Egg Whites:
    - In a large mixing bowl, beat the egg whites with an electric mixer on medium speed until soft peaks form. Add the vanilla extract.
6. Combine the Mixtures:
    - Gradually add the slightly cooled fruit and agar-agar mixture to the beaten egg whites, continuing to beat on medium speed. The mixture should become thick and glossy.
7. Pipe the Zefir:

- Transfer the mixture to a piping bag fitted with a large star tip. Pipe the mixture onto a baking sheet lined with parchment paper, creating spirals or dollops. Alternatively, you can use spoons to drop dollops onto the baking sheet.

8. Dry the Zefir:
    - Let the zefir sit at room temperature for at least 4-6 hours or overnight to dry and set. They should become firm to the touch.
9. Dust with Powdered Sugar:
    - Once the zefir has set, dust them with powdered sugar to prevent sticking. Gently remove them from the parchment paper.

Tips:

- Store zefir in an airtight container at room temperature for up to a week.
- You can experiment with different fruit purees to create various flavors of zefir.
- Ensure the agar-agar is well dissolved to avoid any graininess in the final product.

Enjoy your homemade zefir, a delightful and airy treat!

Chak-Chak

Ingredients:

For the Dough:

- 3 large eggs
- 1 tablespoon granulated sugar
- 1/4 teaspoon salt
- 2 cups all-purpose flour, plus more for dusting
- 1 tablespoon vodka or brandy (optional, helps to make the dough crispier)
- Vegetable oil for frying

For the Syrup:

- 1 cup honey
- 1/2 cup granulated sugar

Instructions:

1. Prepare the Dough:
    - In a large mixing bowl, beat the eggs, granulated sugar, and salt until well combined.
    - Gradually add the flour to the egg mixture, mixing until a soft dough forms. If using, add the vodka or brandy to the dough.
    - Turn the dough out onto a floured surface and knead for about 5-7 minutes until smooth and elastic.
    - Cover the dough with a clean kitchen towel and let it rest for about 30 minutes.
2. Shape the Dough:
    - After the dough has rested, divide it into smaller portions for easier handling.
    - Roll out each portion of dough into a thin sheet, about 1/8 inch thick.
    - Cut the dough into thin strips, then cut the strips into small pieces (about 1/2 inch) to create small dough bits.
3. Fry the Dough:
    - In a deep skillet or pot, heat vegetable oil to 350°F (175°C).
    - Fry the dough pieces in batches until they are golden brown and crispy, about 1-2 minutes per batch. Use a slotted spoon to transfer the fried dough to a paper towel-lined plate to drain excess oil.

4. Make the Syrup:
    - In a medium saucepan, combine the honey and granulated sugar. Heat the mixture over medium heat, stirring constantly, until the sugar dissolves and the mixture begins to boil.
    - Let the syrup boil for about 2-3 minutes, then remove from heat.
5. Combine Dough and Syrup:
    - Place the fried dough pieces in a large mixing bowl.
    - Pour the hot honey syrup over the fried dough pieces and quickly toss to coat evenly.
6. Shape the Chak-Chak:
    - Transfer the coated dough pieces to a serving platter and shape them into a mound or any desired form. Press gently to help them stick together.
7. Cool and Serve:
    - Let the chak-chak cool and set for about 1 hour before serving. It can be garnished with chopped nuts or dried fruits if desired.

Tips:

- Work quickly when mixing the fried dough with the syrup, as the syrup will harden as it cools.
- Ensure the dough pieces are fried evenly for the best texture.
- Store leftover chak-chak in an airtight container at room temperature for up to a week.

Enjoy your homemade chak-chak, a delightful and sweet treat that's perfect for sharing!

Oreshki

Ingredients:

For the Dough:

- 3 large eggs
- 1 tablespoon granulated sugar
- 1/4 teaspoon salt
- 2 cups all-purpose flour, plus more for dusting
- 1 tablespoon vodka or brandy (optional, helps to make the dough crispier)
- Vegetable oil for frying

For the Syrup:

- 1 cup honey
- 1/2 cup granulated sugar

Instructions:

1. Prepare the Dough:
    - In a large mixing bowl, beat the eggs, granulated sugar, and salt until well combined.
    - Gradually add the flour to the egg mixture, mixing until a soft dough forms. If using, add the vodka or brandy to the dough.
    - Turn the dough out onto a floured surface and knead for about 5-7 minutes until smooth and elastic.
    - Cover the dough with a clean kitchen towel and let it rest for about 30 minutes.
2. Shape the Dough:
    - After the dough has rested, divide it into smaller portions for easier handling.
    - Roll out each portion of dough into a thin sheet, about 1/8 inch thick.
    - Cut the dough into thin strips, then cut the strips into small pieces (about 1/2 inch) to create small dough bits.
3. Fry the Dough:
    - In a deep skillet or pot, heat vegetable oil to 350°F (175°C).
    - Fry the dough pieces in batches until they are golden brown and crispy, about 1-2 minutes per batch. Use a slotted spoon to transfer the fried dough to a paper towel-lined plate to drain excess oil.

4. Make the Syrup:
    - In a medium saucepan, combine the honey and granulated sugar. Heat the mixture over medium heat, stirring constantly, until the sugar dissolves and the mixture begins to boil.
    - Let the syrup boil for about 2-3 minutes, then remove from heat.
5. Combine Dough and Syrup:
    - Place the fried dough pieces in a large mixing bowl.
    - Pour the hot honey syrup over the fried dough pieces and quickly toss to coat evenly.
6. Shape the Chak-Chak:
    - Transfer the coated dough pieces to a serving platter and shape them into a mound or any desired form. Press gently to help them stick together.
7. Cool and Serve:
    - Let the chak-chak cool and set for about 1 hour before serving. It can be garnished with chopped nuts or dried fruits if desired.

Tips:

- Work quickly when mixing the fried dough with the syrup, as the syrup will harden as it cools.
- Ensure the dough pieces are fried evenly for the best texture.
- Store leftover chak-chak in an airtight container at room temperature for up to a week.

Enjoy your homemade chak-chak, a delightful and sweet treat that's perfect for sharing!

Oreshki

Ingredients:

For the Dough:

- 2 large eggs
- 1/2 cup granulated sugar
- 1/2 cup unsalted butter, melted
- 1/4 teaspoon salt
- 1 teaspoon vanilla extract
- 1/2 teaspoon baking soda
- 1 tablespoon vinegar or lemon juice (to activate the baking soda)
- 2 1/2 cups all-purpose flour

For the Filling:

- 1 can (14 ounces) sweetened condensed milk, boiled for 2-3 hours to make dulce de leche, or store-bought dulce de leche
- 1/2 cup unsalted butter, softened
- Optional: ground nuts (walnuts, hazelnuts, etc.)

Special Equipment:

- Oreshki mold (either stovetop or electric)

Instructions:

1. Prepare the Dough:
    - In a large mixing bowl, beat the eggs and sugar until well combined and slightly frothy.
    - Add the melted butter, salt, and vanilla extract, and mix until smooth.
    - In a small bowl, combine the baking soda with vinegar or lemon juice, and add to the egg mixture.
    - Gradually add the flour, mixing until a soft dough forms. The dough should be firm enough to shape but still slightly sticky.
2. Shape and Cook the Shells:
    - Preheat the oreshki mold according to the manufacturer's instructions.
    - Take small pieces of dough (about the size of a marble) and place them into the mold. Close the mold and cook according to the manufacturer's

instructions until the shells are golden brown. This usually takes 1-2 minutes per batch.
      - Remove the cooked shells from the mold and let them cool on a wire rack. Repeat with the remaining dough.
  3. Prepare the Filling:
      - In a mixing bowl, beat the softened butter until light and fluffy.
      - Gradually add the dulce de leche and continue to beat until well combined and smooth.
      - If desired, stir in ground nuts for added texture and flavor.
  4. Assemble the Oreshki:
      - Take two cookie shells and fill one half with the dulce de leche mixture.
      - Press the other half gently onto the filling to form a "nut" shape. Be careful not to overfill, as the filling will spread slightly when pressed together.
      - Repeat with the remaining shells and filling.
  5. Serve and Enjoy:
      - Arrange the filled oreshki on a serving platter. They can be served immediately or stored in an airtight container at room temperature for up to a week.

Tips:

- To boil the sweetened condensed milk, place the unopened can in a pot of water, ensuring the can is fully submerged. Simmer for 2-3 hours, adding more water as needed to keep the can covered. Let the can cool completely before opening.
- If you don't have an oreshki mold, you can use a walnut-shaped cookie cutter or another similar mold, though the traditional shape and texture may differ.
- For added flavor, you can dust the assembled oreshki with powdered sugar or cocoa powder before serving.

Enjoy making and sharing these delightful oreshki cookies with family and friends!

Sochnik

Ingredients:

For the Dough:

- 2 large eggs
- 1/2 cup granulated sugar
- 1/2 cup sour cream
- 1/2 cup unsalted butter, melted and cooled
- 1 teaspoon vanilla extract
- 2 1/2 cups all-purpose flour
- 1 teaspoon baking powder
- 1/4 teaspoon salt

For the Filling:

- 1 1/2 cups farmer's cheese (tvorog) or ricotta cheese, well-drained
- 1 large egg yolk
- 1/4 cup granulated sugar
- 1 teaspoon vanilla extract
- 1 tablespoon sour cream
- 1 tablespoon all-purpose flour

For the Egg Wash:

- 1 large egg, beaten with 1 tablespoon of water

Instructions:

1. Prepare the Dough:
     - In a large mixing bowl, whisk together the eggs and sugar until well combined.
     - Add the sour cream, melted butter, and vanilla extract, and mix until smooth.
     - In a separate bowl, whisk together the flour, baking powder, and salt.
     - Gradually add the dry ingredients to the wet ingredients, mixing until a soft dough forms. The dough should be slightly sticky but manageable. If it's too sticky, add a little more flour.
     - Cover the dough with plastic wrap and refrigerate for at least 30 minutes.
2. Prepare the Filling:

- In a medium mixing bowl, combine the farmer's cheese, egg yolk, sugar, vanilla extract, sour cream, and flour. Mix until smooth and well combined. If the mixture seems too loose, you can add a bit more flour to thicken it.
3. Assemble the Sochnik:
    - Preheat the oven to 350°F (175°C) and line a baking sheet with parchment paper.
    - On a floured surface, roll out the dough to about 1/8 inch thickness.
    - Use a round cookie cutter or a glass (about 4 inches in diameter) to cut out circles from the dough.
    - Place a spoonful of the cheese filling in the center of each dough circle.
    - Fold one side of the dough over the filling, but do not seal the edges completely. The edges should be slightly open to expose some of the filling.
    - Place the sochnik on the prepared baking sheet.
4. Bake the Sochnik:
    - Brush the tops of the sochnik with the beaten egg wash.
    - Bake in the preheated oven for 20-25 minutes, or until the pastries are golden brown.
5. Serve:
    - Allow the sochnik to cool slightly on a wire rack before serving. They can be enjoyed warm or at room temperature.

Tips:

- Ensure the farmer's cheese is well-drained to prevent the filling from being too runny.
- You can dust the sochnik with powdered sugar before serving for an extra touch of sweetness.
- Store leftover sochnik in an airtight container at room temperature for up to 2 days or refrigerate for up to a week. Reheat slightly before serving if desired.

Enjoy these delicious homemade sochnik pastries with your favorite cup of tea or coffee!

Tvorozhniki

Ingredients:

- 1 lb (450 g) farmer's cheese (tvorog) or ricotta cheese
- 2 large eggs
- 1/4 cup granulated sugar
- 1 teaspoon vanilla extract
- 1/4 teaspoon salt
- 1/2 cup all-purpose flour, plus more for dusting
- Vegetable oil or butter for frying
- Optional: raisins or other dried fruits

Instructions:

1. Prepare the Cheese Mixture:
    - In a large mixing bowl, combine the farmer's cheese, eggs, sugar, vanilla extract, and salt. Mix until well combined and smooth. If the cheese mixture is too wet, you can strain the cheese through a fine-mesh sieve or cheesecloth.
    - Gradually add the flour, mixing until a soft dough forms. The dough should be slightly sticky but manageable. If you are using raisins or dried fruits, fold them into the dough at this stage.
2. Shape the Pancakes:
    - Dust your hands and a work surface with flour. Take a small portion of the dough (about 2-3 tablespoons) and shape it into a ball. Flatten it slightly to form a thick pancake, about 1/2 inch thick. Repeat with the remaining dough.
    - Lightly coat each pancake with flour to prevent sticking during frying.
3. Fry the Pancakes:
    - In a large skillet, heat a few tablespoons of vegetable oil or butter over medium heat.
    - Fry the tvorozhniki in batches, cooking each side for about 3-4 minutes until golden brown and cooked through. Adjust the heat as necessary to prevent burning. Transfer the cooked pancakes to a paper towel-lined plate to drain excess oil.
4. Serve:

- Serve the tvorozhniki warm, topped with sour cream, fresh berries, honey, or your favorite jam. They can also be dusted with powdered sugar for added sweetness.

Tips:

- Ensure the farmer's cheese is well-drained to achieve the right consistency for the dough.
- If the dough is too sticky to handle, you can refrigerate it for about 30 minutes to make it easier to shape.
- Tvorozhniki can be stored in an airtight container in the refrigerator for up to 3 days. Reheat them in a skillet or microwave before serving.

Enjoy these delicious and creamy tvorozhniki as a comforting breakfast or dessert!

Kulebyaka

Ingredients:

For the Dough:

- 3 1/2 cups all-purpose flour
- 1 cup unsalted butter, cold and cut into small pieces
- 1/2 cup sour cream
- 1/2 cup cold water
- 1 large egg
- 1 teaspoon salt

For the Filling:

- 1 lb (450 g) salmon fillet, skin removed
- 1/2 cup rice, cooked and cooled
- 1 cup mushrooms, finely chopped
- 1 medium onion, finely chopped
- 2 hard-boiled eggs, chopped
- 2 tablespoons butter
- 1/4 cup dill, chopped
- Salt and pepper to taste
- 1 egg, beaten (for egg wash)

Instructions:

1. Prepare the Dough:
    - In a large mixing bowl, combine the flour and salt.
    - Add the cold butter pieces and use a pastry cutter or your fingers to work the butter into the flour until the mixture resembles coarse crumbs.
    - In a small bowl, whisk together the sour cream, cold water, and egg. Add this mixture to the flour and butter mixture.
    - Mix until a dough forms. Turn the dough out onto a floured surface and knead briefly until smooth.
    - Wrap the dough in plastic wrap and refrigerate for at least 1 hour.
2. Prepare the Filling:
    - In a skillet, melt the butter over medium heat. Add the chopped onions and mushrooms, and sauté until soft and golden brown. Season with salt and pepper. Let cool.

- In a large bowl, combine the cooked rice, sautéed mushrooms and onions, chopped hard-boiled eggs, and dill. Mix well and adjust seasoning with salt and pepper.
- Cut the salmon fillet into strips or chunks, depending on your preference.
3. Assemble the Kulebyaka:
    - Preheat the oven to 375°F (190°C). Line a baking sheet with parchment paper.
    - On a floured surface, roll out half of the dough into a large rectangle, about 1/4 inch thick. Place the dough on the prepared baking sheet.
    - Spread half of the rice mixture onto the center of the dough, leaving a border around the edges. Layer the salmon pieces on top of the rice mixture, then top with the remaining rice mixture.
    - Roll out the remaining dough into a rectangle large enough to cover the filling. Place it over the filling and seal the edges by pressing them together. Trim any excess dough.
    - Use a fork or your fingers to crimp the edges. Cut a few slits on top of the pie to allow steam to escape.
    - Brush the top of the pie with the beaten egg.
4. Bake the Kulebyaka:
    - Bake in the preheated oven for 45-50 minutes, or until the crust is golden brown and the filling is heated through.
    - Let the kulebyaka cool for a few minutes before slicing and serving.

Tips:

- You can customize the filling by adding other ingredients such as sautéed spinach, cabbage, or different types of fish.
- Ensure that the filling is well-seasoned, as the rice can absorb a lot of flavors.
- For a more decorative touch, use leftover dough to create patterns or shapes on top of the pie before baking.

Enjoy your delicious and impressive kulebyaka, perfect for a special meal or festive occasion!

Kisel

Ingredients:

- 4 cups (1 liter) water
- 2 cups fresh or frozen berries (such as strawberries, raspberries, or cranberries)
- 1/2 cup granulated sugar (adjust to taste)
- 3 tablespoons potato starch or cornstarch
- 1 teaspoon vanilla extract (optional)

Instructions:

1. Prepare the Fruit Base:
    - In a large saucepan, combine the water and berries. Bring to a boil over medium-high heat, then reduce the heat and simmer for about 10 minutes, until the berries are soft and have released their juices.
    - Remove the saucepan from the heat. If you prefer a smooth kisel, strain the mixture through a fine-mesh sieve to remove the berry seeds and skins, pressing down on the solids to extract as much juice as possible. If you like a chunkier texture, you can skip this step.
2. Sweeten the Juice:
    - Return the strained juice to the saucepan (or keep the unstrained mixture if you prefer). Add the sugar and stir until dissolved. Taste and adjust the sweetness as needed.
3. Thicken the Kisel:
    - In a small bowl, mix the potato starch or cornstarch with a few tablespoons of cold water to create a smooth slurry.
    - Bring the berry mixture to a gentle simmer. Gradually whisk the starch slurry into the simmering berry mixture, stirring constantly to prevent lumps.
    - Continue to cook, stirring constantly, until the kisel thickens and becomes translucent. This should take about 1-2 minutes. Do not let it boil vigorously, as this can break down the starch and cause the kisel to become thin again.
4. Add Flavoring:
    - If desired, stir in the vanilla extract for additional flavor.
5. Serve:

- Pour the kisel into individual serving dishes or a large bowl. Allow it to cool to room temperature, then refrigerate until chilled if you prefer to serve it cold.
- Serve kisel on its own, or with a dollop of cream, a scoop of ice cream, or a sprinkle of fresh berries.

Tips:

- You can use any combination of berries or fruit juices to create different flavors of kisel.
- Adjust the amount of starch depending on whether you prefer a drinkable kisel (less starch) or a pudding-like consistency (more starch).
- For a richer flavor, you can substitute some of the water with fruit juice.

Enjoy this refreshing and versatile dessert that's perfect for any occasion!

Keks

Ingredients:

- 1 cup (2 sticks) unsalted butter, softened
- 1 cup granulated sugar
- 4 large eggs
- 1 teaspoon vanilla extract
- 2 cups all-purpose flour
- 2 teaspoons baking powder
- 1/2 teaspoon salt
- 1/2 cup milk
- 1 cup mixed dried fruits (such as raisins, currants, and chopped dried apricots)
- 1/2 cup chopped nuts (such as walnuts or almonds)
- Zest of 1 lemon or orange (optional)
- 2 tablespoons rum or brandy (optional)
- Powdered sugar for dusting (optional)

Instructions:

1. Prepare the Oven and Pan:
    - Preheat your oven to 350°F (175°C). Grease and flour a loaf pan or a bundt pan.
2. Mix the Dried Fruits:
    - In a small bowl, combine the dried fruits with the rum or brandy (if using). Let them soak while you prepare the batter.
3. Prepare the Batter:
    - In a large mixing bowl, cream the softened butter and granulated sugar together until light and fluffy, about 3-4 minutes.
    - Add the eggs one at a time, beating well after each addition. Stir in the vanilla extract and lemon or orange zest (if using).
    - In a separate bowl, whisk together the flour, baking powder, and salt.
    - Gradually add the dry ingredients to the butter mixture, alternating with the milk, beginning and ending with the dry ingredients. Mix just until combined.
4. Add the Fruits and Nuts:
    - Drain any excess liquid from the dried fruits. Gently fold the dried fruits and chopped nuts into the batter until evenly distributed.
5. Bake the Cake:

- Pour the batter into the prepared pan and smooth the top.
- Bake in the preheated oven for 50-60 minutes, or until a toothpick inserted into the center comes out clean.
- If the top starts to brown too quickly, cover it loosely with aluminum foil.

6. Cool and Serve:
   - Let the cake cool in the pan for about 10 minutes, then turn it out onto a wire rack to cool completely.
   - Once cooled, you can dust the top with powdered sugar before serving.

Tips:

- Ensure the butter is properly softened to achieve a smooth batter.
- Feel free to customize the dried fruits and nuts according to your preference.
- The cake can be stored in an airtight container at room temperature for up to a week, or wrapped well and frozen for longer storage.

Enjoy this classic and comforting keks, perfect with a cup of tea or coffee!

Mazurka

Ingredients:

For the Crust:

- 1 cup (2 sticks) unsalted butter, softened
- 1/2 cup granulated sugar
- 2 large egg yolks
- 2 cups all-purpose flour
- 1/2 teaspoon salt

For the Topping:

- 1/2 cup fruit preserves or jam (apricot, raspberry, or your favorite)
- 1/2 cup mixed nuts (almonds, walnuts, hazelnuts), chopped
- 1/2 cup dried fruits (raisins, currants, apricots), chopped
- 1/4 cup honey
- Powdered sugar for dusting (optional)

Instructions:

1. Prepare the Crust:
    - Preheat your oven to 350°F (175°C). Grease a 9x13-inch baking dish or line it with parchment paper.
    - In a large mixing bowl, cream the softened butter and granulated sugar together until light and fluffy.
    - Add the egg yolks and mix until well combined.
    - Gradually add the flour and salt, mixing until a soft dough forms.
    - Press the dough evenly into the prepared baking dish.
2. Bake the Crust:
    - Bake the crust in the preheated oven for about 15-20 minutes, or until it's lightly golden. Remove from the oven and let it cool slightly.
3. Prepare the Topping:
    - Spread the fruit preserves or jam evenly over the baked crust.
    - Sprinkle the chopped nuts and dried fruits evenly over the jam layer.
    - Drizzle the honey over the top of the nuts and fruits.
4. Bake the Mazurka:
    - Return the baking dish to the oven and bake for an additional 20-25 minutes, or until the topping is golden and bubbly.

5. Cool and Serve:
   - Allow the Mazurka to cool completely in the baking dish.
   - Once cooled, you can dust the top with powdered sugar if desired.
   - Cut into squares or bars and serve.

Tips:

- You can customize the toppings with your favorite combinations of nuts and dried fruits.
- For a different flavor profile, try using different types of fruit preserves or jams.
- Store the Mazurka in an airtight container at room temperature for up to a week.

Enjoy this delicious and versatile dessert, perfect for sharing with family and friends!

Gogol-Mogol

Ingredients:

- 2 large eggs
- 2 tablespoons granulated sugar (adjust to taste)
- 1/2 cup milk
- 1/2 teaspoon vanilla extract (optional)
- Ground cinnamon or nutmeg for garnish (optional)

Instructions:

1. Prepare the Eggs:
    - In a small saucepan, whisk together the eggs and sugar until well combined.
2. Heat the Mixture:
    - Place the saucepan over low heat and gradually add the milk while whisking continuously. Be careful not to scramble the eggs.
    - Continue to cook and stir the mixture gently until it thickens slightly and reaches your desired consistency. This should take about 5-7 minutes. The mixture should be smooth and creamy, but not boiling.
3. Flavor and Serve:
    - If using, stir in the vanilla extract for additional flavor.
    - Pour the Gogol-Mogol into serving cups or mugs.
    - Optionally, sprinkle ground cinnamon or nutmeg on top for garnish.
4. Enjoy Warm:
    - Serve the Gogol-Mogol immediately while still warm for a comforting treat.

Tips:

- Adjust the amount of sugar according to your taste preference. You can also substitute honey or other sweeteners if desired.
- For a richer flavor, you can use half-and-half or cream instead of milk.
- Experiment with different flavorings such as almond extract, orange zest, or a splash of rum or brandy for an adult version.
- Be sure to whisk the eggs and sugar thoroughly to ensure a smooth mixture without any lumps.

Gogol-Mogol is a simple and cozy dessert that's perfect for warming up on chilly days or enjoying as a sweet treat any time of year!

Ruzheiki

Ingredients:

- 1 cup all-purpose flour
- 2 large eggs
- 1 cup milk
- 1/4 teaspoon salt
- 2 tablespoons unsalted butter, melted
- Vegetable oil for frying

Instructions:

1. Prepare the Batter:
    - In a mixing bowl, whisk together the flour and salt.
    - In a separate bowl, beat the eggs, then whisk in the milk until well combined.
    - Gradually add the egg and milk mixture to the flour, whisking continuously to avoid lumps.
    - Stir in the melted butter and mix until the batter is smooth. Let the batter rest for about 15-30 minutes at room temperature to allow the gluten to relax.
2. Cook the Ruzheiki:
    - Heat a non-stick skillet or crepe pan over medium heat. Lightly grease the skillet with vegetable oil.
    - Pour a small ladleful of batter into the center of the skillet, swirling it around to spread the batter thinly and evenly across the bottom of the pan.
    - Cook the ruzheiki for about 1-2 minutes, or until the edges begin to lift and the bottom is golden brown.
    - Use a spatula to flip the ruzheiki and cook for another 1-2 minutes on the other side until lightly golden.
3. Serve Warm:
    - Transfer the cooked ruzheiki to a plate and cover with a clean kitchen towel to keep warm.
    - Repeat the process with the remaining batter, greasing the skillet as needed.
    - Serve the ruzheiki warm with your choice of toppings, such as sour cream, jam, honey, caviar, smoked salmon, or a sprinkle of powdered sugar.

Tips:

- Adjust the thickness of the batter by adding more or less milk to achieve your desired consistency.
- To keep the ruzheiki warm while you cook the rest, you can place them on a baking sheet in a warm oven (around 200°F or 90°C).
- If you prefer a sweeter version, you can add a little sugar to the batter.
- Experiment with different fillings and toppings to create both sweet and savory variations of ruzheiki.

Enjoy these delicious and versatile Russian pancakes as a delightful breakfast or snack!

Baranki

Ingredients:

- 3 cups all-purpose flour
- 1 cup warm water
- 1 tablespoon granulated sugar
- 1 teaspoon active dry yeast
- 1 teaspoon salt
- 1 egg, beaten (for egg wash)
- Sesame seeds, poppy seeds, or coarse salt (for topping, optional)

Instructions:

1. Activate the Yeast:
    - In a small bowl, combine the warm water, sugar, and yeast. Stir gently and let it sit for about 5-10 minutes, or until the mixture becomes frothy.
2. Make the Dough:
    - In a large mixing bowl, combine the flour and salt. Make a well in the center and pour in the yeast mixture.
    - Gradually incorporate the flour into the wet ingredients, mixing until a dough forms.
    - Turn the dough out onto a lightly floured surface and knead for about 5-7 minutes, or until the dough is smooth and elastic.
3. Shape the Baranki:
    - Divide the dough into small portions, about the size of a golf ball.
    - Roll each portion into a rope, about 5-6 inches long. Join the ends to form a ring shape and pinch the ends together to seal.
4. Boil the Baranki (Optional):
    - In a large pot, bring water to a boil. Once boiling, reduce the heat to a simmer.
    - Working in batches, carefully drop the baranki into the simmering water and cook for about 1-2 minutes, flipping them halfway through.
    - Remove the baranki from the water using a slotted spoon and place them on a clean kitchen towel to drain excess water.
5. Bake the Baranki:
    - Preheat your oven to 375°F (190°C). Line a baking sheet with parchment paper.

- Place the boiled or unboiled baranki onto the prepared baking sheet, leaving some space between each one.
- Brush the tops of the baranki with beaten egg wash and sprinkle with sesame seeds, poppy seeds, or coarse salt, if desired.
- Bake in the preheated oven for 20-25 minutes, or until the baranki are golden brown and cooked through.

6. Cool and Serve:
    - Let the baranki cool on a wire rack before serving.
    - Enjoy them plain or with butter, cheese, or your favorite spread.

Tips:

- Baranki can be stored in an airtight container at room temperature for a few days. You can also freeze them for longer storage.
- Feel free to customize the toppings or add flavors to the dough, such as garlic powder, onion flakes, or herbs, to create different variations of baranki.

Enjoy these simple and delicious Russian bread rings as a tasty snack or accompaniment to your favorite beverage!

Sukhariki

Ingredients:

- 4 cups stale bread (such as white or wheat sandwich bread), cut into bite-sized cubes
- 3 tablespoons olive oil or melted butter
- 1-2 cloves garlic, minced (optional)
- 1 teaspoon dried herbs (such as oregano, thyme, or rosemary)
- Salt and pepper to taste

Instructions:

1. Preheat the Oven:
    - Preheat your oven to 350°F (175°C). Line a baking sheet with parchment paper or aluminum foil for easy cleanup.
2. Prepare the Bread:
    - Cut the stale bread into bite-sized cubes, about 1/2 to 1 inch in size. You can remove the crusts if desired, but it's not necessary.
3. Season the Sukhariki:
    - In a large mixing bowl, combine the olive oil or melted butter with the minced garlic (if using), dried herbs, salt, and pepper. Mix well to combine.
    - Add the bread cubes to the bowl and toss gently to coat evenly with the seasoned oil or butter mixture. Make sure each piece is coated on all sides.
4. Toast the Sukhariki:
    - Spread the seasoned bread cubes in a single layer on the prepared baking sheet.
    - Bake in the preheated oven for 10-15 minutes, or until the sukhariki are golden brown and crispy, stirring halfway through to ensure even browning.
    - Keep an eye on them towards the end of the baking time to prevent burning.
5. Cool and Serve:
    - Remove the baking sheet from the oven and let the sukhariki cool completely on the pan.
    - Once cooled, transfer the crispy bread cubes to an airtight container for storage.

- Enjoy the sukhariki as a snack on their own, or use them as a crunchy topping for soups, salads, or even dips.

Tips:

- You can customize the seasoning of the sukhariki to your taste. Try adding grated Parmesan cheese, paprika, onion powder, or any other spices you like.
- Make sure to use stale bread for this recipe, as fresh bread may become too soft when toasted.
- Store the sukhariki in an airtight container at room temperature for up to a week. If they start to lose their crispiness, you can reheat them in the oven for a few minutes before serving.

Enjoy these homemade sukhariki as a tasty and crunchy snack or topping!

Marmelad

Ingredients:

- 4 cups fruit puree or juice (such as apple, strawberry, raspberry, apricot, or a combination)
- 2 cups granulated sugar
- 1/4 cup lemon juice
- 1 packet (about 2 tablespoons) powdered fruit pectin (optional, for firmer texture)
- Butter or oil for greasing the pan

Instructions:

1. Prepare the Fruit Puree:
   - If using whole fruits, wash them thoroughly and remove any stems, seeds, or pits.
   - Place the fruits in a blender or food processor and blend until smooth to make the fruit puree. You can strain the puree through a fine-mesh sieve to remove any solids if desired.
2. Cook the Marmelad:
   - In a large, heavy-bottomed saucepan, combine the fruit puree, granulated sugar, and lemon juice.
   - If using powdered fruit pectin for a firmer texture, sprinkle it over the fruit mixture and stir to combine.
   - Place the saucepan over medium heat and bring the mixture to a boil, stirring frequently to dissolve the sugar.
   - Reduce the heat to low and simmer the mixture, stirring occasionally, until it thickens and reaches the desired consistency. This can take anywhere from 30 minutes to 1 hour, depending on the fruits used and the desired thickness of the marmelad.
3. Test for Doneness:
   - To test if the marmelad is ready, spoon a small amount onto a chilled plate. If it sets and holds its shape, it's done. If it's still too runny, continue to cook for a few more minutes and test again.
4. Pour and Set:
   - Once the marmelad is ready, immediately pour it into a greased baking dish or mold, spreading it out into an even layer.
   - Let the marmelad cool completely at room temperature, then cover and refrigerate for several hours or overnight to allow it to set firm.

5. Cut and Serve:
    - Once the marmelad has set, use a sharp knife to cut it into squares or rectangles.
    - Serve the marmelad on its own as a sweet treat, or use it as a topping for toast, pancakes, or yogurt.

Tips:

- You can customize the flavor of the marmelad by using different fruits or adding spices such as cinnamon, vanilla, or ginger.
- If you prefer a smoother texture, you can puree the fruit mixture in a blender after cooking and before pouring it into the mold.
- Store the marmelad in an airtight container in the refrigerator for up to two weeks. You can also freeze it for longer storage.

Enjoy making and indulging in this delightful homemade marmelad!

Kulebyaka with Sweet Filling

Ingredients:

For the Dough:

- 2 1/2 cups all-purpose flour
- 1 cup unsalted butter, cold and cubed
- 1/2 cup sour cream
- 1 teaspoon salt

For the Sweet Filling:

- 3 cups fruit filling of your choice (e.g., apple, cherry, apricot, or a combination)
- 1/4 cup granulated sugar (adjust to taste)
- 1 tablespoon cornstarch
- 1 teaspoon ground cinnamon (optional)
- 1 egg, beaten (for egg wash)

Instructions:

1. Prepare the Dough:
    - In a large mixing bowl, combine the flour and salt.
    - Add the cold cubed butter to the flour mixture and use a pastry cutter or your fingers to work it into the flour until the mixture resembles coarse crumbs.
    - Add the sour cream and mix until the dough comes together. If the dough is too dry, you can add a little more sour cream, 1 tablespoon at a time.
    - Shape the dough into a ball, wrap it in plastic wrap, and refrigerate for at least 30 minutes.
2. Prepare the Sweet Filling:
    - In a mixing bowl, combine the fruit filling, granulated sugar, cornstarch, and ground cinnamon (if using). Mix until well combined.
3. Assemble the Kulebyaka:
    - Preheat your oven to 375°F (190°C). Line a baking sheet with parchment paper.
    - Divide the chilled dough into two equal portions. Roll out one portion of the dough on a floured surface into a large rectangle, about 1/4 inch thick.
    - Transfer the rolled-out dough onto the prepared baking sheet.

- Spread the sweet filling evenly over the rolled-out dough, leaving a border around the edges.
- Roll out the remaining portion of the dough into a rectangle of similar size and thickness. Place it over the sweet filling to cover it completely.
- Pinch the edges of the dough together to seal the filling inside. Use a fork to crimp the edges for a decorative finish.
- Use a sharp knife to make a few small slits on the top of the Kulebyaka to allow steam to escape.
- Brush the top of the Kulebyaka with beaten egg wash for a golden finish.

4. Bake the Kulebyaka:
   - Bake in the preheated oven for 35-40 minutes, or until the crust is golden brown and the filling is bubbling.
   - If the top starts to brown too quickly, you can cover it loosely with aluminum foil.

5. Cool and Serve:
   - Let the Kulebyaka cool on the baking sheet for a few minutes before transferring it to a wire rack to cool completely.
   - Once cooled, slice the Kulebyaka into portions and serve warm or at room temperature.

Tips:

- You can use any fruit filling you like for the sweet filling. Homemade or store-bought pie fillings work well.
- Feel free to add chopped nuts or raisins to the sweet filling for extra texture and flavor.
- Serve the sweet Kulebyaka on its own or with a dollop of whipped cream or a scoop of vanilla ice cream for a delicious dessert.

Enjoy this delightful Russian pastry with a sweet twist!

Sushki

Ingredients:

- 2 cups all-purpose flour
- 1/2 cup warm water
- 1 teaspoon active dry yeast
- 1 tablespoon granulated sugar
- 1/2 teaspoon salt
- 1 egg, beaten (for egg wash)
- Optional toppings: poppy seeds, sesame seeds, coarse salt

Instructions:

1. Activate the Yeast:
    - In a small bowl, combine the warm water, sugar, and yeast. Stir gently and let it sit for about 5-10 minutes, or until the mixture becomes frothy.
2. Make the Dough:
    - In a large mixing bowl, combine the flour and salt.
    - Make a well in the center of the flour mixture and pour in the activated yeast mixture.
    - Stir until a dough forms, then knead the dough on a floured surface for about 5-7 minutes, or until it becomes smooth and elastic.
3. Shape the Sushki:
    - Divide the dough into small portions and roll each portion into a long rope, about 1/2 inch thick.
    - Cut each rope into smaller pieces, about 3-4 inches long.
    - Shape each piece into a small ring, pressing the ends together firmly to seal. You can also twist the ends together for a more traditional sushki shape.
4. Boil the Sushki:
    - Preheat your oven to 350°F (175°C).
    - Bring a large pot of water to a boil. Once boiling, reduce the heat to a simmer.
    - Working in batches, carefully drop the sushki into the simmering water and cook for about 2-3 minutes. They should float to the surface when they're done.
    - Remove the boiled sushki from the water using a slotted spoon and place them on a clean kitchen towel to drain excess water.

5. Bake the Sushki:
   - Place the boiled sushki on a baking sheet lined with parchment paper.
   - Brush the tops of the sushki with beaten egg wash and sprinkle with your choice of toppings, such as poppy seeds, sesame seeds, or coarse salt.
   - Bake in the preheated oven for 20-25 minutes, or until the sushki are golden brown and crispy.
6. Cool and Serve:
   - Let the sushki cool on the baking sheet for a few minutes before transferring them to a wire rack to cool completely.
   - Once cooled, store the sushki in an airtight container at room temperature for up to a week.

Tips:

- You can adjust the size of the sushki according to your preference.
- Experiment with different toppings to customize the flavor of the sushki.
- Enjoy the sushki as a crunchy snack on their own, or serve them with tea or coffee.

These homemade sushki are perfect for enjoying as a snack or for sharing with friends and family!

Tula Gingerbread

Ingredients:

For the Dough:

- 3 cups all-purpose flour
- 1/2 teaspoon baking soda
- 1 teaspoon ground cinnamon
- 1 teaspoon ground ginger
- 1/2 teaspoon ground cloves
- 1/2 teaspoon ground nutmeg
- 1/2 cup unsalted butter, softened
- 1/2 cup granulated sugar
- 1/2 cup honey
- 1 large egg

For the Glaze:

- 1 cup powdered sugar
- 1-2 tablespoons water or lemon juice
- Decorative toppings (such as colored sugar, sprinkles, or edible pearls)

Instructions:

1. Prepare the Dough:
    - In a mixing bowl, sift together the flour, baking soda, cinnamon, ginger, cloves, and nutmeg. Set aside.
    - In a separate bowl, cream together the softened butter and granulated sugar until light and fluffy.
    - Add the honey and egg to the butter mixture, and beat until well combined.
    - Gradually add the dry ingredients to the wet ingredients, mixing until a soft dough forms.
    - Wrap the dough in plastic wrap and refrigerate for at least 1 hour, or until firm.
2. Roll and Cut the Cookies:
    - Preheat your oven to 350°F (175°C). Line baking sheets with parchment paper.
    - On a floured surface, roll out the chilled dough to about 1/4 inch thickness.

- Use cookie cutters to cut out shapes from the dough. You can use traditional gingerbread shapes like hearts, stars, or circles, or use special Tula gingerbread molds if you have them.
      - Place the cut-out cookies onto the prepared baking sheets, leaving some space between each cookie.
3. Bake the Cookies:
      - Bake the cookies in the preheated oven for 10-12 minutes, or until the edges are lightly golden brown.
      - Remove the cookies from the oven and let them cool on the baking sheets for a few minutes before transferring them to a wire rack to cool completely.
4. Decorate with Glaze:
      - In a small bowl, whisk together the powdered sugar and water or lemon juice to make a smooth glaze.
      - Once the cookies are completely cooled, drizzle or spread the glaze over the top of each cookie.
      - Decorate the glazed cookies with colored sugar, sprinkles, or edible pearls while the glaze is still wet.
5. Allow the Glaze to Set:
      - Let the cookies sit at room temperature for about 1 hour, or until the glaze is completely set.
6. Enjoy:
      - Serve the Tula gingerbread cookies with tea or coffee, or package them up as gifts for friends and family.

Tips:

- Tula gingerbread cookies can be stored in an airtight container at room temperature for up to a week.
- Feel free to experiment with different shapes and decorations to make your gingerbread cookies unique.

Enjoy making and sharing these delicious Tula gingerbread cookies!

Far Breton

Ingredients:

- 1 cup pitted prunes or dried fruit of your choice
- 1 cup all-purpose flour
- 1/2 cup granulated sugar
- Pinch of salt
- 4 large eggs
- 2 cups whole milk
- 1/4 cup dark rum (optional)
- Butter for greasing the baking dish
- Powdered sugar for dusting (optional)

Instructions:

1. Prepare the Prunes:
    - Place the prunes in a small bowl and cover them with warm water. Let them soak for about 15-20 minutes to soften. Drain and pat dry with paper towels.
2. Preheat the Oven:
    - Preheat your oven to 350°F (175°C). Grease a 9-inch round baking dish with butter.
3. Make the Batter:
    - In a mixing bowl, whisk together the flour, granulated sugar, and salt.
    - In a separate bowl, beat the eggs, then gradually whisk in the milk until well combined.
    - Gradually add the wet ingredients to the dry ingredients, whisking until you have a smooth batter.
    - Stir in the dark rum if using.
4. Assemble and Bake:
    - Arrange the soaked prunes evenly in the bottom of the greased baking dish.
    - Pour the batter over the prunes, ensuring they are evenly distributed.
    - Bake in the preheated oven for 45-55 minutes, or until the Far Breton is set and golden brown on top. It should be slightly jiggly in the center but set around the edges.
5. Cool and Serve:
    - Allow the Far Breton to cool in the baking dish for about 15-20 minutes.

- Dust the top with powdered sugar if desired.
- Slice and serve the Far Breton warm or at room temperature.

Tips:

- You can customize the recipe by using different dried fruits such as apricots, cherries, or raisins.
- If you prefer a non-alcoholic version, you can omit the rum or substitute it with vanilla extract.
- Far Breton is often enjoyed as a dessert but can also be served for breakfast or brunch.
- Leftover Far Breton can be stored in the refrigerator for a few days. It can be enjoyed cold or gently reheated before serving.

Enjoy this classic French dessert with its velvety texture and rich flavors!

Pirog with Sweet Filling

Ingredients:

For the Dough:

- 2 1/4 teaspoons (1 packet) active dry yeast
- 1/4 cup warm water (110°F/45°C)
- 1 cup warm milk (110°F/45°C)
- 1/2 cup granulated sugar
- 1/3 cup unsalted butter, melted
- 2 large eggs
- 4 cups all-purpose flour
- 1/2 teaspoon salt

For the Sweet Filling:

- 2 cups fruit filling of your choice (e.g., apple, cherry, apricot, or a combination)
- 1/4 cup granulated sugar (adjust to taste)
- 1 tablespoon cornstarch
- 1 teaspoon ground cinnamon (optional)

For the Glaze:

- 1 cup powdered sugar
- 2-3 tablespoons milk or water
- 1/2 teaspoon vanilla extract (optional)

Instructions:

1. Prepare the Dough:
    - In a small bowl, sprinkle the yeast over the warm water. Let it sit for about 5 minutes, or until it becomes frothy.
    - In a large mixing bowl, combine the warm milk, granulated sugar, melted butter, and eggs. Add the activated yeast mixture and mix until well combined.
    - Gradually add the flour and salt to the wet ingredients, stirring until a soft dough forms.
    - Turn the dough out onto a floured surface and knead for about 5-7 minutes, or until it becomes smooth and elastic. Add more flour if needed to prevent sticking.

- Place the dough in a greased bowl, cover with a clean kitchen towel, and let it rise in a warm place for about 1-2 hours, or until doubled in size.
2. Prepare the Sweet Filling:
    - In a mixing bowl, combine the fruit filling, granulated sugar, cornstarch, and ground cinnamon (if using). Mix until well combined.
3. Assemble the Pirog:
    - Preheat your oven to 350°F (175°C). Grease a baking sheet or line it with parchment paper.
    - Punch down the risen dough and divide it into two equal portions.
    - Roll out one portion of the dough into a large rectangle on a floured surface, about 1/4 inch thick.
    - Transfer the rolled-out dough to the prepared baking sheet.
    - Spread the sweet filling evenly over the rolled-out dough, leaving a border around the edges.
    - Roll out the remaining portion of the dough into a rectangle of similar size and thickness. Place it over the sweet filling to cover it completely.
    - Pinch the edges of the dough together to seal the filling inside. Use a fork to crimp the edges for a decorative finish.
    - Use a sharp knife to make a few small slits on the top of the pirog to allow steam to escape.
4. Bake the Pirog:
    - Bake in the preheated oven for 30-35 minutes, or until the pirog is golden brown and cooked through.
5. Prepare the Glaze:
    - In a small bowl, whisk together the powdered sugar, milk or water, and vanilla extract (if using) to make a smooth glaze.
6. Glaze and Serve:
    - Once the pirog is baked and cooled slightly, drizzle the glaze over the top.
    - Slice and serve the pirog warm or at room temperature.

Tips:

- You can customize the filling by using different fruits, jams, or preserves according to your preference.
- Feel free to add chopped nuts or raisins to the filling for extra texture and flavor.
- Pirog is best enjoyed fresh on the day it's made, but leftovers can be stored in an airtight container at room temperature for up to 2 days.

Enjoy this delicious pirog with a sweet filling as a delightful dessert or treat!

Solozhenka

Ingredients:

- 1 can (14 oz) sweetened condensed milk
- 1/2 cup granulated sugar
- 2 tablespoons unsalted butter
- Pinch of salt (optional)

Instructions:

1. Prepare the Ingredients:
    - Open the can of sweetened condensed milk and pour it into a heavy-bottomed saucepan.
    - Add the granulated sugar and butter to the saucepan.
2. Cook the Mixture:
    - Place the saucepan over medium heat and stir the mixture continuously with a wooden spoon or silicone spatula.
    - Cook the mixture for about 15-20 minutes, or until it thickens and turns a light caramel color. Keep stirring to prevent the mixture from burning or sticking to the bottom of the pan.
    - If you're using a candy thermometer, the temperature should reach about 230°F (110°C).
3. Test for Doneness:
    - To test if the solozhenka is ready, drop a small amount of the mixture into a bowl of cold water. It should form a soft ball that holds its shape but is still pliable. If it's too soft, continue cooking for a few more minutes.
4. Cool and Serve:
    - Once the solozhenka reaches the desired consistency, remove the saucepan from the heat and let it cool slightly.
    - Pour the solozhenka into a greased or parchment paper-lined dish or tray.
    - Let it cool completely at room temperature, then cut it into squares or rectangles.
    - Serve the solozhenka as a sweet treat or dessert.

Tips:

- You can add a pinch of salt to enhance the flavor of the solozhenka.
- Feel free to customize the recipe by adding chopped nuts, vanilla extract, or other flavorings.

- Store the solozhenka in an airtight container at room temperature for up to a week. You can also refrigerate it for longer storage.

Enjoy making and indulging in this creamy and delicious Russian dessert!

Gnezdo

Ingredients:

- 200g shredded wheat biscuits (or similar cereal)
- 200g chocolate (milk, dark, or a combination)
- 100g unsalted butter
- 1/4 cup honey or golden syrup
- Optional: chopped nuts, dried fruits, or coconut flakes for decoration
- Mini chocolate eggs or candy eggs for garnish

Instructions:

1. Prepare the Shredded Wheat:
    - Crush the shredded wheat biscuits into small pieces. You can do this by placing them in a plastic bag and crushing them with a rolling pin or pulsing them in a food processor.
2. Melt the Chocolate and Butter:
    - In a heatproof bowl set over a pot of simmering water (or in the microwave using short intervals), melt the chocolate and butter together, stirring until smooth.
    - Stir in the honey or golden syrup until well combined.
3. Mix the Ingredients:
    - Add the crushed shredded wheat to the melted chocolate mixture. Stir until the shredded wheat is fully coated in chocolate.
4. Form the Nests:
    - Take small portions of the mixture and shape them into nest-like forms on a baking sheet lined with parchment paper. Create an indentation in the center of each nest to resemble a nest shape.
    - If desired, press chopped nuts, dried fruits, or coconut flakes onto the surface of the nests for decoration.
5. Chill and Decorate:
    - Place the baking sheet in the refrigerator and chill the nests for about 30 minutes, or until they are firm and set.
    - Once the nests are chilled, gently place mini chocolate eggs or candy eggs in the center of each nest to resemble eggs in a bird's nest.
6. Serve and Enjoy:
    - Serve the gnezdo nests as a delightful Easter treat or dessert.

- Store any leftovers in an airtight container in the refrigerator for up to a week.

Tips:

- You can customize the gnezdo nests by adding different mix-ins or toppings, such as chopped nuts, dried fruits, coconut flakes, or sprinkles.
- For a more decadent version, you can drizzle melted chocolate over the top of the nests for extra decoration.
- Experiment with different types of chocolate and cereal to find your favorite combination.

Enjoy making and indulging in these adorable and delicious gnezdo nests!

Prianik

Ingredients:

For the Dough:

- 2 cups all-purpose flour
- 1 teaspoon baking soda
- 1 teaspoon ground cinnamon
- 1/2 teaspoon ground cloves
- 1/2 teaspoon ground nutmeg
- 1/4 teaspoon ground ginger
- Pinch of salt
- 1/2 cup unsalted butter, softened
- 1/2 cup granulated sugar
- 1/2 cup honey
- 2 large eggs

For the Glaze:

- 1 cup powdered sugar
- 1-2 tablespoons water or lemon juice
- 1/2 teaspoon vanilla extract (optional)

Instructions:

1. Prepare the Dough:
    - Preheat your oven to 350°F (175°C). Line baking sheets with parchment paper.
    - In a mixing bowl, sift together the flour, baking soda, cinnamon, cloves, nutmeg, ginger, and salt. Set aside.
    - In a separate bowl, cream together the softened butter and granulated sugar until light and fluffy.
    - Add the honey and eggs to the butter mixture, one at a time, beating well after each addition.
    - Gradually add the dry ingredients to the wet ingredients, mixing until a soft dough forms.
2. Shape the Prianiki:
    - Flour your hands and a clean work surface. Take small portions of the dough and shape them into balls or patties, about 1 inch in diameter.

- Place the shaped pryaniki onto the prepared baking sheets, leaving some space between each cookie.
3. Bake the Prianiki:
    - Bake in the preheated oven for 10-12 minutes, or until the pryaniki are lightly golden brown and set.
    - Remove the cookies from the oven and let them cool on the baking sheets for a few minutes before transferring them to a wire rack to cool completely.
4. Prepare the Glaze:
    - In a small bowl, whisk together the powdered sugar, water or lemon juice, and vanilla extract (if using) to make a smooth glaze.
    - Once the pryaniki are completely cooled, drizzle the glaze over the top of each cookie.
5. Allow the Glaze to Set:
    - Let the glazed pryaniki sit at room temperature for about 1 hour, or until the glaze is completely set.
6. Serve and Enjoy:
    - Serve the pryaniki as a sweet treat or dessert with tea or coffee.
    - Store any leftovers in an airtight container at room temperature for up to a week.

Tips:

- Feel free to customize the recipe by adding chopped nuts, dried fruits, or chocolate chips to the dough for extra flavor and texture.
- You can also experiment with different spices and flavorings to suit your taste preferences.
- Adjust the thickness of the glaze by adding more or less water or lemon juice until you reach your desired consistency.

Enjoy making and savoring these delightful Russian pryaniki!

Kisel with Berries

Ingredients:

- 2 cups fresh or frozen berries (such as strawberries, raspberries, blueberries, or a combination)
- 4 cups water
- 1/2 cup granulated sugar (adjust to taste)
- 3-4 tablespoons cornstarch or potato starch
- 1/4 cup cold water
- 1 teaspoon vanilla extract (optional)
- Fresh mint leaves for garnish (optional)

Instructions:

1. Prepare the Berries:
   - If using fresh berries, rinse them under cold water and remove any stems or debris. If using frozen berries, thaw them according to the package instructions.
2. Cook the Berries:
   - In a saucepan, combine the berries, 4 cups of water, and granulated sugar. Bring the mixture to a boil over medium heat, stirring occasionally.
3. Thicken the Kisel:
   - In a small bowl, mix the cornstarch or potato starch with 1/4 cup of cold water until smooth and lump-free.
   - Slowly pour the starch mixture into the boiling berry mixture, stirring constantly to prevent lumps from forming.
   - Cook the kisel for an additional 2-3 minutes, or until it thickens to your desired consistency.
4. Add Flavoring (Optional):
   - Stir in the vanilla extract if using, to add extra flavor to the kisel. You can also add a squeeze of lemon juice for a hint of acidity if desired.
5. Cool and Serve:
   - Remove the saucepan from the heat and let the kisel cool slightly before serving.
   - Serve the kisel warm in individual bowls or glasses, or chill it in the refrigerator for a few hours until cold.
6. Garnish and Enjoy:

- Garnish the kisel with fresh mint leaves or additional berries before serving, if desired.
- Enjoy the kisel as a refreshing dessert or snack.

Tips:

- You can adjust the sweetness of the kisel by adding more or less sugar according to your taste preferences.
- For a smoother texture, you can strain the cooked berries through a fine mesh sieve to remove any seeds before thickening the kisel with starch.
- Experiment with different combinations of berries and flavorings to create your own unique variations of kisel.

Enjoy this delightful and refreshing berry kisel!

Lazy Vareniki

Ingredients:

For the Dough:

- 2 cups all-purpose flour
- 1 cup sour cream
- 1 egg
- 1/2 teaspoon salt

For the Filling:

- 1 cup cottage cheese or farmer's cheese
- 1 egg
- 2 tablespoons granulated sugar (for sweet version) or salt (for savory version)
- Optional: vanilla extract, cinnamon, or other flavorings for sweet version; chopped herbs or sautéed onions for savory version

Instructions:

1. Prepare the Dough:
    - In a mixing bowl, combine the flour, sour cream, egg, and salt. Mix until a soft dough forms. If the dough is too sticky, add a little more flour. If it's too dry, add a little more sour cream.
2. Prepare the Filling:
    - In a separate bowl, mix together the cottage cheese, egg, sugar or salt, and any optional flavorings or additions.
3. Assemble the Lazy Vareniki:
    - Preheat your oven to 350°F (175°C). Grease a baking dish with butter or cooking spray.
    - Roll out the dough on a floured surface into a rectangle about 1/4 inch thick.
    - Spread the filling evenly over the dough, leaving a small border around the edges.
    - Carefully roll up the dough, jelly-roll style, to encase the filling.
    - Slice the rolled-up dough into rounds, about 1 inch thick.
4. Bake the Lazy Vareniki:
    - Arrange the sliced lazy vareniki in the greased baking dish.

- Bake in the preheated oven for 25-30 minutes, or until the lazy vareniki are golden brown and cooked through.

5. **Serve and Enjoy:**
    - Serve the lazy vareniki hot, either as a main dish or as a dessert.
    - For a sweet version, you can sprinkle powdered sugar over the top before serving.
    - Enjoy your delicious and easy-to-make lazy vareniki!

Tips:

- You can customize the filling and dough according to your preferences. For a savory version, try adding cooked meat, sautéed onions, or herbs to the filling. For a sweet version, experiment with different types of cheese, fruits, or jams.
- Lazy vareniki can be served on their own or with sour cream, yogurt, or fruit compote for dipping or drizzling.
- Leftover lazy vareniki can be stored in the refrigerator for a few days and reheated in the oven or microwave before serving.

Enjoy this simple and comforting dish!

Baked Apples with Honey

Ingredients:

- 4 large apples (such as Granny Smith, Honeycrisp, or Gala)
- 1/4 cup chopped nuts (such as walnuts, pecans, or almonds), optional
- 1/4 cup raisins or dried cranberries, optional
- 2 tablespoons unsalted butter, melted
- 2 tablespoons honey
- 1 teaspoon ground cinnamon
- 1/4 teaspoon ground nutmeg
- Pinch of salt
- Vanilla ice cream or whipped cream, for serving (optional)

Instructions:

1. Preheat the Oven:
    - Preheat your oven to 375°F (190°C).
2. Prepare the Apples:
    - Wash the apples and pat them dry. Using an apple corer or a small paring knife, core the apples, making sure to leave the bottom intact to create a well for the filling.
    - If desired, use a sharp knife to score a shallow ring around the middle of each apple to prevent them from bursting during baking.
3. Make the Filling:
    - In a small bowl, mix together the chopped nuts (if using), raisins or dried cranberries (if using), melted butter, honey, cinnamon, nutmeg, and a pinch of salt until well combined.
4. Fill the Apples:
    - Place the cored apples in a baking dish or on a parchment-lined baking sheet.
    - Spoon the filling mixture into the center of each apple, packing it tightly.
5. Bake the Apples:
    - Bake the apples in the preheated oven for 25-30 minutes, or until they are tender and the filling is bubbling.
    - If the tops of the apples start to brown too quickly, cover them loosely with aluminum foil.
6. Serve:

- Remove the baked apples from the oven and let them cool slightly before serving.
- Serve the baked apples warm, optionally topped with a scoop of vanilla ice cream or a dollop of whipped cream.

7. Enjoy:
    - Enjoy these delicious baked apples with honey as a comforting dessert or snack!

Tips:

- You can customize the filling by adding other ingredients such as chopped dried fruits, shredded coconut, or spices like ginger or cloves.
- If you prefer a sweeter filling, you can increase the amount of honey or add a sprinkle of brown sugar over the top of the apples before baking.
- Leftover baked apples can be stored in the refrigerator for a few days and reheated in the microwave before serving.

These baked apples with honey are a cozy and comforting treat that's sure to be a hit with family and friends!

Sweet Syrniki with Raisins

Ingredients:

- 2 cups farmer's cheese (tvorog or quark), well-drained
- 2 large eggs
- 1/4 cup granulated sugar
- 1/2 teaspoon vanilla extract
- 1/4 cup all-purpose flour, plus more for dusting
- 1/4 cup raisins
- Vegetable oil, for frying
- Sour cream, honey, or fruit preserves, for serving (optional)

Instructions:

1. Prepare the Farmer's Cheese:
    - If your farmer's cheese is wet, place it in a fine mesh strainer set over a bowl and let it drain for about 30 minutes to remove excess moisture.
2. Soak the Raisins:
    - Place the raisins in a small bowl and cover them with hot water. Let them soak for about 10-15 minutes to plump up. Then, drain the raisins and pat them dry with paper towels.
3. Mix the Batter:
    - In a large mixing bowl, combine the drained farmer's cheese, eggs, granulated sugar, and vanilla extract. Mix until well combined.
    - Gradually add the flour to the mixture, stirring until a thick batter forms.
    - Gently fold in the soaked and drained raisins.
4. Shape the Syrniki:
    - Dust your hands with flour to prevent sticking. Take a small portion of the batter and shape it into a small pancake or patty, about 2-3 inches in diameter and 1/2 inch thick. Repeat with the remaining batter.
5. Fry the Syrniki:
    - Heat a skillet or frying pan over medium heat and add enough vegetable oil to coat the bottom.
    - Once the oil is hot, carefully place the shaped syrniki in the pan, leaving some space between them to allow for flipping.
    - Cook the syrniki for 2-3 minutes on each side, or until they are golden brown and cooked through. You may need to adjust the heat as needed to prevent burning.

6. Serve:
    - Transfer the cooked syrniki to a plate lined with paper towels to drain any excess oil.
    - Serve the syrniki warm, optionally topped with sour cream, honey, or fruit preserves.

Tips:

- You can customize the syrniki by adding other mix-ins such as chopped nuts, chocolate chips, or dried fruits.
- If you prefer a lighter version, you can bake the syrniki in the oven instead of frying them. Simply place them on a parchment-lined baking sheet and bake at 375°F (190°C) for about 15-20 minutes, or until golden brown.
- Leftover syrniki can be stored in the refrigerator for a few days and reheated in the microwave or oven before serving.

Enjoy these sweet and delicious syrniki with raisins as a delightful breakfast or dessert!

Sweet Curd Dumplings

Ingredients:

For the Dough:

- 2 cups all-purpose flour
- 1/2 teaspoon salt
- 1/2 cup warm water
- 1 large egg

For the Filling:

- 2 cups farmer's cheese (tvorog or quark), well-drained
- 1/4 cup granulated sugar
- 1/2 teaspoon vanilla extract
- Optional: lemon zest, cinnamon, or raisins for added flavor

For Serving:

- Sour cream
- Fruit preserves or compote
- Powdered sugar (optional)

Instructions:

1. Prepare the Dough:
    - In a large mixing bowl, combine the flour and salt. Make a well in the center and add the warm water and egg. Mix until a dough forms.
    - Knead the dough on a floured surface for about 5 minutes, or until it becomes smooth and elastic. Cover the dough with a clean kitchen towel and let it rest for 15-20 minutes.
2. Prepare the Filling:
    - In another bowl, mix together the farmer's cheese, granulated sugar, vanilla extract, and any optional flavorings or additions such as lemon zest, cinnamon, or raisins. Mix until well combined.
3. Shape the Dumplings:
    - Roll out the rested dough on a floured surface to about 1/8 inch thickness. Use a round cookie cutter or a glass to cut out circles of dough.

- Place a spoonful of the cheese filling in the center of each dough circle. Fold the dough over the filling to create a half-moon shape, then pinch the edges to seal.
4. Cook the Dumplings:
    - Bring a large pot of salted water to a gentle boil. Carefully drop the dumplings into the boiling water, working in batches to avoid overcrowding.
    - Cook the dumplings for 3-4 minutes, or until they float to the surface and are cooked through. Use a slotted spoon to remove them from the water and transfer them to a plate.
5. Serve:
    - Serve the sweet curd dumplings warm, topped with sour cream and fruit preserves or compote. You can also sprinkle them with powdered sugar for extra sweetness, if desired.
6. Enjoy:
    - Enjoy these delicious sweet curd dumplings as a comforting dessert or treat!

Tips:

- Make sure to drain the farmer's cheese well to remove excess moisture and prevent the filling from being too wet.
- Feel free to customize the filling with your favorite flavors and additions, such as different spices, nuts, or dried fruits.
- Leftover dumplings can be stored in an airtight container in the refrigerator for a few days. Reheat them gently in the microwave or steam them before serving.

These sweet curd dumplings are a classic Eastern European dessert that's sure to delight your taste buds!

Bird's Milk Cake

Ingredients:

For the Sponge Cake:

- 4 large eggs
- 1 cup granulated sugar
- 1 cup all-purpose flour
- 1 teaspoon baking powder
- 1/4 cup milk
- 1 teaspoon vanilla extract

For the Creamy Mousse Layer:

- 2 cups milk
- 1/2 cup granulated sugar
- 1/4 cup cornstarch
- 4 large egg whites
- 1/2 cup granulated sugar
- 1 teaspoon vanilla extract
- 1 envelope (about 2 1/2 teaspoons) unflavored gelatin
- 1/4 cup cold water
- 1 cup heavy cream

For the Chocolate Glaze:

- 1 cup semisweet chocolate chips
- 1/2 cup heavy cream

Instructions:

1. Prepare the Sponge Cake:
    - Preheat your oven to 350°F (175°C). Grease and flour a 9x13-inch baking pan.
    - In a large mixing bowl, beat the eggs and granulated sugar until light and fluffy.
    - Gradually add the flour and baking powder to the egg mixture, mixing until well combined.
    - Stir in the milk and vanilla extract until smooth.
    - Pour the batter into the prepared baking pan and spread it out evenly.

- Bake in the preheated oven for 20-25 minutes, or until a toothpick inserted into the center comes out clean.
- Remove the sponge cake from the oven and let it cool completely in the pan.

2. Prepare the Creamy Mousse Layer:
   - In a saucepan, combine the milk and granulated sugar for the mousse layer. Heat over medium heat until the sugar is dissolved and the mixture is hot but not boiling.
   - In a separate bowl, whisk together the cornstarch and egg whites until smooth.
   - Gradually pour the hot milk mixture into the egg mixture, whisking constantly.
   - Return the mixture to the saucepan and cook over medium heat, stirring constantly, until thickened.
   - Remove the saucepan from the heat and stir in the vanilla extract.
   - In a small bowl, sprinkle the gelatin over the cold water and let it sit for a few minutes to soften.
   - Stir the softened gelatin into the hot milk mixture until dissolved. Let the mixture cool to room temperature.
   - In a separate bowl, whip the heavy cream until stiff peaks form. Gently fold the whipped cream into the cooled milk mixture until smooth and well combined.

3. Assemble the Cake:
   - Once the sponge cake has cooled, spread the creamy mousse layer evenly over the top.
   - Refrigerate the cake for at least 2-3 hours, or until the mousse layer is set.

4. Prepare the Chocolate Glaze:
   - In a microwave-safe bowl, combine the chocolate chips and heavy cream for the glaze. Microwave in 30-second intervals, stirring after each interval, until the chocolate is melted and the mixture is smooth.
   - Let the chocolate glaze cool slightly.

5. Finish and Serve:
   - Pour the chocolate glaze over the chilled cake, spreading it out evenly with a spatula.
   - Return the cake to the refrigerator for another 1-2 hours, or until the glaze is set.
   - Once set, slice the bird's milk cake into squares and serve chilled.

Tips:

- You can customize the cake by adding a layer of fruit preserves or fresh fruit between the sponge cake and the mousse layer.
- For a lighter mousse layer, you can fold in some whipped egg whites before adding the whipped cream.
- Store any leftover cake in the refrigerator for up to 3-4 days.

Enjoy this delicious and indulgent bird's milk cake as a special dessert for any occasion!

Cottage Cheese Pancakes

Ingredients:

- 2 cups cottage cheese (farmer's cheese or tvorog)
- 2 large eggs
- 1/4 cup granulated sugar
- 1 teaspoon vanilla extract
- 1/2 cup all-purpose flour
- 1/2 teaspoon baking powder
- Pinch of salt
- Vegetable oil, for frying
- Optional toppings: sour cream, jam, honey, fresh berries, powdered sugar

Instructions:

1. Prepare the Cottage Cheese:
    - If the cottage cheese is too wet, place it in a fine mesh strainer set over a bowl and let it drain for about 15-20 minutes to remove excess moisture.
2. Mix the Batter:
    - In a large mixing bowl, combine the drained cottage cheese, eggs, granulated sugar, and vanilla extract. Mix until well combined.
    - In a separate bowl, sift together the flour, baking powder, and salt. Gradually add the dry ingredients to the cottage cheese mixture, stirring until smooth.
3. Fry the Pancakes:
    - Heat a non-stick skillet or griddle over medium heat. Add a small amount of vegetable oil to coat the bottom of the skillet.
    - Once the skillet is hot, drop spoonfuls of the pancake batter onto the skillet, spreading them out slightly with the back of the spoon to form pancakes.
    - Cook the pancakes for 2-3 minutes on each side, or until golden brown and cooked through. You may need to adjust the heat as needed to prevent burning.
    - Remove the pancakes from the skillet and place them on a plate lined with paper towels to drain any excess oil.
4. Serve:
    - Serve the cottage cheese pancakes warm, topped with your favorite toppings such as sour cream, jam, honey, fresh berries, or powdered sugar.

- - Enjoy these delicious and fluffy pancakes as a satisfying breakfast or snack!

Tips:

- For extra flavor, you can add a sprinkle of cinnamon or lemon zest to the pancake batter.
- You can make the pancakes smaller or larger depending on your preference.
- Leftover pancakes can be stored in an airtight container in the refrigerator for a few days. Reheat them in the microwave or toaster oven before serving.

These cottage cheese pancakes are sure to become a favorite in your breakfast rotation!

Kasha with Berries

Ingredients:

- 1 cup buckwheat groats (kasha)
- 2 cups water
- Pinch of salt
- 1 cup fresh or frozen berries (such as strawberries, blueberries, raspberries, or a mix)
- 2 tablespoons honey or maple syrup (optional)
- 1/4 cup chopped nuts or seeds (such as almonds, walnuts, or sunflower seeds) for topping (optional)

Instructions:

1. Prepare the Buckwheat Groats:
   - Rinse the buckwheat groats under cold water in a fine mesh strainer to remove any debris.
   - In a saucepan, combine the rinsed buckwheat groats, water, and a pinch of salt.
   - Bring the water to a boil over high heat, then reduce the heat to low and cover the saucepan with a lid.
   - Simmer the buckwheat groats for about 10-12 minutes, or until the water is absorbed and the groats are tender. Remove the saucepan from the heat and let it sit, covered, for a few minutes.
2. Cook the Berries:
   - While the buckwheat groats are cooking, prepare the berries. If using fresh berries, rinse them under cold water and pat them dry. If using frozen berries, thaw them according to the package instructions.
   - In a small saucepan, heat the berries over medium heat until they start to release their juices and soften, about 5-7 minutes. Stir in the honey or maple syrup, if using, to sweeten the berries.
3. Assemble the Dish:
   - Fluff the cooked buckwheat groats with a fork and divide them evenly among serving bowls.
   - Spoon the cooked berries and their juices over the buckwheat groats.
4. Serve:
   - Serve the kasha with berries warm, optionally topped with chopped nuts or seeds for added texture and flavor.

- Enjoy this wholesome and satisfying dish for breakfast or as a healthy snack!

Tips:

- Feel free to customize the dish by adding other ingredients such as sliced bananas, chopped apples, or dried fruits to the cooked buckwheat groats.
- Adjust the sweetness of the dish by adding more or less honey or maple syrup to the berries.
- Leftover kasha with berries can be stored in an airtight container in the refrigerator for a few days. Reheat it in the microwave or on the stovetop before serving.

Enjoy this delicious and nutritious kasha with berries for a wholesome start to your day!

Apple Pie (Yablochny Pirog)

Ingredients:

For the Crust:

- 2 1/2 cups all-purpose flour
- 1 cup unsalted butter, cold and cut into small cubes
- 1/4 cup granulated sugar
- 1/4 teaspoon salt
- 1 large egg
- 2-4 tablespoons ice water

For the Filling:

- 5-6 large apples (such as Granny Smith or Golden Delicious), peeled, cored, and thinly sliced
- 1/2 cup granulated sugar
- 2 tablespoons all-purpose flour
- 1 teaspoon ground cinnamon
- 1/4 teaspoon ground nutmeg
- 1 tablespoon lemon juice
- 2 tablespoons unsalted butter, cut into small cubes

For Assembly:

- 1 large egg, beaten (for egg wash)
- Granulated sugar (for sprinkling)

Instructions:

1. Prepare the Crust:
    - In a large mixing bowl, combine the flour, sugar, and salt. Add the cold cubed butter and mix until the mixture resembles coarse crumbs.
    - In a small bowl, beat the egg and add it to the flour mixture. Gradually add the ice water, 1 tablespoon at a time, mixing until the dough comes together.
    - Divide the dough into two equal portions, shape each portion into a disk, wrap them in plastic wrap, and refrigerate for at least 1 hour.
2. Prepare the Filling:

    - In a separate bowl, combine the sliced apples, granulated sugar, flour, cinnamon, nutmeg, and lemon juice. Toss until the apples are evenly coated.
3. Assemble the Pie:
    - Preheat your oven to 375°F (190°C). Prepare a 9-inch pie dish by greasing it lightly.
    - On a lightly floured surface, roll out one disk of the chilled dough into a circle large enough to fit into the bottom and up the sides of the pie dish. Carefully transfer the dough to the pie dish and trim any excess dough from the edges.
    - Spread the apple filling evenly into the prepared pie crust. Dot the top of the filling with the cubed butter.
4. Top the Pie:
    - Roll out the second disk of chilled dough into a circle large enough to cover the pie. Place the dough over the filling and press the edges of the top and bottom crusts together to seal. Trim any excess dough and crimp the edges with a fork or your fingers to create a decorative border.
    - Cut a few slits in the top crust to allow steam to escape during baking. Brush the top crust with beaten egg and sprinkle with granulated sugar.
5. Bake the Pie:
    - Place the assembled pie on a baking sheet to catch any drips. Bake in the preheated oven for 45-50 minutes, or until the crust is golden brown and the filling is bubbly.
    - If the edges of the crust start to brown too quickly, cover them loosely with aluminum foil.
6. Serve:
    - Allow the pie to cool slightly before serving. Serve warm or at room temperature, optionally with a scoop of vanilla ice cream or a dollop of whipped cream.

Enjoy this classic Yablochny Pirog with its comforting aroma and delicious flavor!

Sweet Bread Rolls (Bulochki)

Ingredients:

For the Dough:

- 4 cups all-purpose flour
- 1/2 cup granulated sugar
- 1 packet (2 1/4 teaspoons) active dry yeast
- 1 cup warm milk
- 1/2 cup unsalted butter, melted
- 2 large eggs
- 1 teaspoon vanilla extract
- 1/2 teaspoon salt

For the Filling (Optional):

- Fruit preserves, poppy seed filling, sweetened cottage cheese, or Nutella

For Glazing:

- 1 egg, beaten (for egg wash)
- Granulated sugar or powdered sugar (for dusting)

Instructions:

1. Activate the Yeast:
    - In a small bowl, dissolve the yeast and a pinch of sugar in warm milk. Let it sit for about 5-10 minutes until frothy.
2. Make the Dough:
    - In a large mixing bowl, combine the flour, sugar, and salt. Make a well in the center and add the yeast mixture, melted butter, eggs, and vanilla extract.
    - Mix the ingredients until a soft dough forms. If the dough is too sticky, add more flour, one tablespoon at a time, until it comes together.
    - Turn the dough out onto a floured surface and knead it for about 5-7 minutes, or until it becomes smooth and elastic.
3. First Rise:
    - Place the dough in a greased bowl, cover it with a clean kitchen towel or plastic wrap, and let it rise in a warm place for about 1-1.5 hours, or until doubled in size.

4. **Shape the Rolls:**
   - Punch down the risen dough and divide it into equal-sized portions. Shape each portion into a ball.
   - If using fillings, flatten each ball into a disc, spoon a small amount of filling into the center, and pinch the edges to seal. Roll it into a ball again.
5. **Second Rise:**
   - Place the shaped rolls on a baking sheet lined with parchment paper, leaving some space between them. Cover them with a clean kitchen towel and let them rise for another 30-45 minutes, or until they double in size.
6. **Bake the Rolls:**
   - Preheat your oven to 350°F (175°C). Brush the risen rolls with beaten egg (egg wash).
   - Bake in the preheated oven for 15-20 minutes, or until golden brown and cooked through. If the tops start to brown too quickly, cover them loosely with aluminum foil.
7. **Glaze and Serve:**
   - Remove the rolls from the oven and let them cool slightly on a wire rack.
   - Dust the warm rolls with granulated sugar or powdered sugar before serving.

Enjoy these delicious sweet bread rolls (bulochki) warm with a cup of tea or coffee for a delightful treat! You can also experiment with different fillings to suit your taste preferences.

Creamy Semolina Porridge

Ingredients:

- 1 cup semolina flour
- 4 cups milk (whole milk or your preferred type)
- 1/4 cup granulated sugar (adjust to taste)
- 1 teaspoon vanilla extract or vanilla sugar
- Pinch of salt
- Optional toppings: butter, ground cinnamon, fresh berries, jam, or honey

Instructions:

1. Prepare the Semolina:
    - In a saucepan, bring the milk to a gentle simmer over medium heat. Add a pinch of salt.
2. Add Semolina:
    - Gradually sprinkle the semolina flour into the simmering milk, stirring constantly with a whisk to prevent lumps from forming.
3. Cook the Porridge:
    - Continue stirring the mixture over medium-low heat for about 5-7 minutes, or until the porridge thickens to your desired consistency. Be careful as the porridge will thicken quickly.
    - Stir in the granulated sugar and vanilla extract or vanilla sugar. Adjust the sweetness according to your taste preferences.
4. Serve:
    - Once the porridge reaches your desired consistency and sweetness, remove it from the heat.
    - Serve the creamy semolina porridge warm in bowls.
5. Optional Toppings:
    - Garnish the creamy semolina porridge with a pat of butter, a sprinkle of ground cinnamon, fresh berries, a dollop of jam, or a drizzle of honey, if desired.
6. Enjoy:
    - Enjoy the creamy semolina porridge as a comforting breakfast or snack!

Tips:

- For a richer flavor, you can use a combination of milk and water or add a splash of cream to the porridge.

- Stir the porridge constantly while cooking to prevent it from sticking to the bottom of the saucepan and forming lumps.
- Adjust the thickness of the porridge by adding more milk if it becomes too thick or by cooking it longer if it's too thin.
- Customize the porridge with your favorite toppings such as nuts, dried fruits, or chocolate chips.

Creamy semolina porridge is a simple and satisfying breakfast that's sure to warm you up on chilly mornings. Feel free to adjust the sweetness and toppings to suit your taste preferences!

Russian Tea Cookies

Ingredients:

- 1 cup unsalted butter, softened
- 1/2 cup powdered sugar, plus extra for coating
- 1 teaspoon vanilla extract
- 2 cups all-purpose flour
- 1 cup finely chopped nuts (such as pecans, walnuts, or almonds)

Instructions:

1. Preheat the Oven:
    - Preheat your oven to 350°F (175°C). Line a baking sheet with parchment paper or lightly grease it.
2. Cream Butter and Sugar:
    - In a large mixing bowl, cream together the softened butter and powdered sugar until light and fluffy.
3. Add Vanilla and Flour:
    - Mix in the vanilla extract until well combined.
    - Gradually add the flour, mixing until the dough comes together. Fold in the chopped nuts until evenly distributed.
4. Shape the Dough:
    - Take small portions of the dough and roll them into 1-inch balls. Place the balls on the prepared baking sheet, spacing them about 1 inch apart.
5. Bake:
    - Bake the cookies in the preheated oven for 12-15 minutes, or until they are set but not browned.
6. Cool:
    - Remove the cookies from the oven and let them cool on the baking sheet for a few minutes.
7. Coat in Powdered Sugar:
    - While the cookies are still warm, roll them in powdered sugar until evenly coated. You can also dust them with powdered sugar using a sifter if preferred.
8. Cool Completely:
    - Transfer the coated cookies to a wire rack to cool completely.
9. Re-Coat (Optional):

- - Once the cookies have cooled completely, you can roll them in powdered sugar again for an extra coating.
10. Serve:
- Serve the Russian tea cookies on a platter and enjoy with a cup of tea or coffee.

These Russian tea cookies are perfect for holiday gatherings, afternoon tea parties, or as a sweet treat any time of the year. They store well in an airtight container at room temperature for several days, although they're so delicious they may not last that long!

Honey Cake

Ingredients:

For the Cake Layers:

- 4 cups all-purpose flour
- 4 large eggs
- 1 cup granulated sugar
- 1 cup honey
- 1/2 cup unsalted butter, softened
- 1 teaspoon baking soda
- 1 teaspoon baking powder
- 1 teaspoon ground cinnamon
- Pinch of salt

For the Filling:

- 2 cups sour cream
- 1 cup heavy cream
- 1 cup powdered sugar
- 1 teaspoon vanilla extract

For Assembly:

- Honey for drizzling
- Chopped nuts or grated chocolate (optional, for garnish)

Instructions:

1. Make the Cake Layers:
    - Preheat your oven to 350°F (175°C). Grease and flour a 9-inch round cake pan.
    - In a large mixing bowl, beat the eggs and sugar together until pale and fluffy. Add the softened butter and honey, and mix until well combined.
    - In a separate bowl, sift together the flour, baking soda, baking powder, cinnamon, and salt. Gradually add the dry ingredients to the wet ingredients, mixing until a smooth dough forms.
    - Divide the dough into 8 equal portions. Roll out each portion into a thin circle, about 9 inches in diameter.

- Place each circle of dough onto the prepared cake pan and prick it all over with a fork. Bake in the preheated oven for about 8-10 minutes, or until lightly golden brown. Remove from the oven and let them cool completely.
2. Make the Filling:
    - In a large mixing bowl, whip the heavy cream until stiff peaks form. In another bowl, mix together the sour cream, powdered sugar, and vanilla extract until smooth. Gently fold the whipped cream into the sour cream mixture until well combined.
3. Assemble the Cake:
    - Place one cake layer on a serving plate or cake stand. Spread a layer of the filling over the cake layer. Repeat with the remaining cake layers and filling, stacking them on top of each other.
4. Finish the Cake:
    - Once all the cake layers are stacked, spread the remaining filling over the top and sides of the cake to cover it completely.
    - Drizzle honey over the top of the cake and garnish with chopped nuts or grated chocolate, if desired.
5. Chill and Serve:
    - Refrigerate the cake for at least 4 hours, or overnight, to allow the flavors to meld and the cake to set.
    - Slice and serve the honey cake chilled. Enjoy!

This honey cake is perfect for special occasions or as a sweet treat to enjoy with family and friends. Its unique flavor and moist texture make it a favorite dessert in Russian cuisine.

Lemon Kulich

Ingredients:

For the Dough:

- 4 cups all-purpose flour
- 1/2 cup granulated sugar
- 1/2 cup unsalted butter, melted
- 3/4 cup warm milk
- 2 large eggs, beaten
- 1 package (2 1/4 teaspoons) active dry yeast
- Zest of 2 lemons
- 1/4 cup lemon juice
- 1 teaspoon vanilla extract
- Pinch of salt

For the Glaze:

- 1 cup powdered sugar
- 2-3 tablespoons lemon juice

For Decoration (Optional):

- Candied lemon peel
- Slivered almonds
- Powdered sugar for dusting

Instructions:

1. Activate the Yeast:
    - In a small bowl, dissolve the yeast and a pinch of sugar in warm milk. Let it sit for about 5-10 minutes until frothy.
2. Make the Dough:
    - In a large mixing bowl, combine the flour, sugar, lemon zest, and salt. Make a well in the center and add the melted butter, beaten eggs, activated yeast mixture, lemon juice, and vanilla extract.
    - Mix the ingredients until a soft dough forms. If the dough is too sticky, add more flour, one tablespoon at a time, until it comes together.
    - Knead the dough on a floured surface for about 5-7 minutes, or until it becomes smooth and elastic.

3. First Rise:
   - Place the dough in a greased bowl, cover it with a clean kitchen towel or plastic wrap, and let it rise in a warm place for about 1-1.5 hours, or until doubled in size.
4. Shape the Kulich:
   - Punch down the risen dough and divide it into equal-sized portions. Shape each portion into a tall cylinder and place it in a greased and floured kulich mold or tall cylindrical pan. Cover the molds with a clean kitchen towel and let them rise for another 30-45 minutes.
5. Bake:
   - Preheat your oven to 350°F (175°C). Bake the kulich in the preheated oven for 30-40 minutes, or until golden brown and cooked through. If the tops start to brown too quickly, cover them loosely with aluminum foil.
6. Make the Glaze:
   - In a small bowl, whisk together the powdered sugar and lemon juice until smooth. Adjust the consistency by adding more powdered sugar or lemon juice as needed.
7. Glaze and Decorate:
   - Once the kulich is baked and cooled slightly, brush the glaze over the top of each kulich. Decorate with candied lemon peel and slivered almonds, if desired.
8. Serve:
   - Dust the lemon kulich with powdered sugar before serving. Slice and enjoy this delicious citrusy bread with tea or coffee.

This lemon kulich is a delightful addition to your Easter celebration or any special occasion. Its bright flavor and fluffy texture make it a favorite among family and friends.

www.ingramcontent.com/pod-product-compliance
Lightning Source LLC
LaVergne TN
LVHW081557060526
838201LV00054B/1933